AT the start of the year, twenty-five vehicles were outstanding from batches linked to 2015 contracts, as well as six LTs for the route 168 conversion. Most of the stragglers entered service in January, but it was slow going. Among those that did make it onto the road was the last of Arriva's E400H Citys for route 78.

Above: Sutton garage received six of the thirty Volvo/Gemini 3s ordered by Go-Ahead for the contract renewals of routes 155 and 93 in 2015. The two morning peak-hour journeys worked by Merton buses on the 93 continued in the new year, alongside the 'genuine' Sutton vehicles delivered in January. From that group, this is WHV105 at the northbound Wimbledon station stop on the 13th.

Below: Other stragglers could be found running around the same one-way system – the remaining 10.8 metre E200s for Merton to convert route 164. From the nine delivered in January, this is SE284 crossing the hump over the main line railway at the start of the journey to Sutton.

What Happened Next

THE last of Arriva's first batch Enviro 400H Citys, HA19, entered service on January 30th. During the month, one or two of the new arrivals began to appear each day on route 106, leaving Ash Grove's fairly-ancient VLWs to fill the gaps on the 78. The practice continued through February but HAs rarely strayed onto the garage's third double-deck route, the 254.

Later in the year, an order for a second batch was announced for Arriva London South's takeover of route 333 in January 2017.

To recap, the City is a development of the ADL Enviro400 MMC, influenced by TfL's desire for a 'London look' vehicle - hence the design mods, red interior mouldings and a new seat moquette nodding towards that of the original Routemaster.

See page 58 for CT Plus's introduction of the type onto route 26, and page 66 for Wrightbus's version of a London-look vehicle.

Below: After a Christmas truce, Go-Ahead's War on Scanias resumed with the withdrawal and sale of the ELS type from route 42. By January the 8th, several other single-deckers had begun to appear, especially SOEs displaced from Merton by the new Enviro200s.

The vehicle allocation had moved back to Camberwell from Mandela Way in October 2014, so any of the garage's allocation was likely to appear post-ELS, even the odd Electrocity normally found on route 360. By the summer, the daily diet was LDP type Dart Pointers until the route's upgrade to double-deckers at contract renewal (see Sept/October section.)

The photo shows a line of three at the Liverpool Street stand headed by LDP257. We used to train-spot off this bridge in the 1960s, long before the present 'tomb' was constructed.

Contents

Introduction

WELCOME to the South London edition of Red All Over - an approach dictated by the huge number of contract renewals and changes on the unfashionable side of the river in 2016.

Geographical bias aside, there was a noticeable change of emphasis in the ebb and flow of London's red buses as the year unfolded - not least a 'falling out of love' with the New Routemaster following Boris's departure as mayor in May. After LTs had distorted the new vehicle picture since 2012, the comparatively small number entering service in this twelve-month period allowed a different kind of normality to surface.

In practice that meant lots more Wright Geminis and ADL Enviros, alongside a substantial invasion of new kit from north Africa . . . but with Swedish roots. The common denominator was the much-admired Volvo hybrid chassis, which appears to be taking over as the 'weapon of choice' in the battle to save us from air pollution. In the same battle, the Chinese BYD company scored a notable victory by converting the Red Arrow routes to electric technology.

All of these events and changes are covered in detail in my version of the extended caption, alongside one-off features to illustrate the diversity of the London scene. 2016 was another intensely busy time, with 125 new contracts and almost a thousand new vehicles entering service. To fit everything in, the extra pages added to last year's edition have been retained.

Acknowledgements: Thanks to Arriva, Go-Ahead and Stagecoach for keeping up the generous flow of information that publications like ours depend on. A belated thank you also to Alexander Dennis for arranging our factory visits. Some of the photos appear in this edition to illustrate the Volvo article.

Positive comments from regular readers have been as welcome as ever, and I thank them once again for their encouragement.

David Maxey
Surrey, England
January 2017

Photographs by the author except where shown

Cover: The year's new bus (partly) was the MCV EvoSeti married to the omnipresent Volvo B5L hybrid chassis at a purpose-built factory in Egypt. Go-Ahead ordered eighty-five of this combination for new contracts, like the 185. MHV68 restarts from Vauxhall bus station on an unusually bright November day.

Frontispiece: More than three hundred vehicles changed garages on the night of July 1st/2nd, mostly the residents of Rainham transferring to a new home at River Road, Barking. Sneaking under the wire almost unnoticed in this melée of movement was route 77, which left Merton garage after more than eighty years, taking with it a dedicated batch of Presidents and the four Enviro400s, E276-80, ordered against the last

contract renewal in 2013. One of the quartet pauses outside Lambeth Palace still showing its old garage code (the bus, not the palace).

Below: After various appearances by demonstrators, Optare finally loaned its Metrodecker design to a London operator for trials in daily service. OM1 started work at Bexleyheath on 2nd August and mostly kept to the 486, running alongside Wright's early StreetDeck WSD1. Here's the Optare in a July line-up with HA16 and LT2 at West Ham garage, a special event at which several vehicles were displayed.

Back Cover: Nostalgia for south Londoners of a certain age – the dome of St Stockwell's with an early Titan parked beneath. The London Bus Museum's RTL139 waits to return home at the end of the open day.

Contract Change: London Central (BX) to Arriva KT (DT) – 23.1.16
Type Change: Volvo B9TL/Eclipse Gemini to ADL E40D/Enviro400 [from T301-331]

229

Above: Along with the 422, the route 229 contract was last renewed in January 2011 with a batch of new Volvo B9/Gemini 2s, WVL350-385. The last six were soon transferred to Camberwell to top up the conversion from bendybus of route 12, but the rest formed a common-user pool at Bexleyheath for the next five years. This is WVL354 on a southbound journey at Knee Hill, Abbey Wood.

Arriva ordered thirty-one 'classic' Enviros (i.e. the old body design, but with Euro 6 engine spec) and numbered them in the London series, which had reached T287 with the small batch delivered to South Croydon in 2013. It was thought originally that the TfL routes of Arriva Shires and Arriva Kent Thameside would be absorbed into Arriva London North and South from 1st January – hence the fleet numbers - but the paper transfer happened later, when extra O' Licences came through.

THE January contracts all fell due on the same date – the 23rd – as did February's – the 6th. The first group created a whirlpool of interest in south-east London, the second did not – in south-east London or anywhere else.

In the week before the contract change, several of the new intake were tried out on Dartford's route 160, itself converted to Enviro400s on the cusp of 2011/12. The thirteen buses in that batch conveniently filled the blanks from T288-T300 when renumbering finally began. *Below:* A nearly-new T307 roars past Bexleyheath trolleybus depot.

Twenty-two new vehicles appeared on January the 23rd, ten running for the first time on Dartford routes. Two arrived much later (T320/326) and entered service several weeks after the rest.

Contract Renewal: Arriva KT (DT) - 23.1.16
Type Change: DB250LF/Pulsar Gemini to ADL E40D/Enviro400
[from T301-331]

492

The 492 connects the residents of Bexley and Bexleyheath with the Bluewater Shoppers' Paradise (as well as residents of Sidcup who like longer bus rides) and first ran in 1988 with single-deckers. London Central (Bexleyheath garage) operated the route at the turn of the century, but it passed to Kent Thameside in 2004. This is the second contract renewal, after five years and seven years, so Arriva must be doing something right.

Above: The 'country DWs' have been on the route since new; here's a back-lit 6218 on the outskirts of Dartford.

As this was a renewal rather than an operator change, there was less urgency to get new buses out on a fixed date. The 492 's passengers enjoyed the odd one in the early weeks, but had to wait until mid-February for the full conversion. The last of the E400s entered service on 10th March.

Fall-Out:

In theory, the loss of the 229 rendered more than twenty vehicles redundant at Bexleyheath, but you would never have known that from the pattern of the first week after the contract change. Every one of the Volvo B9s made it onto a route, as the garage rotated its fleet through the 89, 132, 401, 422 and 486, as well as the school journeys. It couldn't last, of course; after clearing out a handful of older types (PVL, WVL), there were still far too many spares. At close of play on January 28th, the lowest-numbered of the batch – WVL350-357 - were taken off the road and transferred to New Cross. From Monday, 1st February, they began to appear on the 321, but straying onto other routes soon became commonplace.

WVL360/2 transferred to Camberwell, WVL361 reappeared on Peckham's 63, WVL363 went to Mandela Way for route 1. WVL364 was taken out of service in mid-journey, dumping its passengers at Royal Standard only ten minutes after leaving North Greenwich. It eventually resurfaced at Stockwell. The extract from London Vehicle Finder shows the sudden end to 364's Bexleyheath career. At least the garage provided a substitute bus to take passengers forward.

Vehicle GAL WVL364 (LX60DWP) has been used as follows

Route	Date	From	Until
19	19-02-2016	08:10	12:54
422	10-02-2016	07:30	11:30

Most interesting of all were the two vehicles transferred to Northumberland Park, WVL358/9. They were pretty much ring-fenced as the permanent motive power for school route 616 but only provided the morning journeys, finishing their day's work at Edmonton Bus Station by 0830. Occasionally, one or the other would work a return trip on a Friday afternoon, but that was it. Despite expectations, neither ventured out on front-line routes during any of the school holidays . . . until half-term at the beginning of June when both appeared without warning on the 191, 259, or 476. So, opposite page, the rare sight of WVL358 at the Manor House crossroads two days into its week-long stint collecting Oyster fares from grown-ups.

The fall-out at Dartford following the 492's conversion was limited but predictable. The garage's seven DAF/Pulsar Geminis – 6213-9, all '53' reg - were withdrawn progressively during February.

Contract Change: Stagecoach Selkent (PD) to Arriva KT (DT) - 23.1.16
Vehicle Change: E200 Dart/Enviro200 to similar 'existing vehicles'

469

The 469's new contract was another of those oddities where a route changes operator but ends up with the same vehicle type as before, prompting the question 'What was the point?' (other than TfL paying a lower contract price for the next five years, obviously). In this particular case, the replacements weren't even new, prompting the same question again. Oh well; here's a Stagecoach bus before the change – 36273, a 10.2 metre E200 Dart built in 2011, at the Queen Elizabeth Hospital Main Entrance stop. The route shares a stand with two others opposite the Queen Elizabeth Hospital West Entrance stop.

Above: One of Arriva's sizeable collection of Wright Cadets, 3945, at the Bexleyheath Market Place/Clock Tower stop. This is from the 9.4 metre batch delivered in 2004, which were still working the route when the contract came up for renewal in 2016. After the MMC conversion, the oldest six – 3945-50, all of them '53' reg – were stood down.

I wouldn't normally devote a whole page to a single-deck conversion, but this was only the second order for MMC single-deckers for a TfL route. However as the year unfolded, the type proliferated alarmingly.

The B13's new buses weren't available on the contract date, so the Cadets enjoyed an extra few weeks of banging around the country roads of Kent. ENR1 entered service on 4th February, along with ENR6, and the rest followed within ten days.

Below: The first of the batch at the Friswell Place bus stand in Bexleyheath after a driver training run from Dartford garage. The new vehicles are similar in length to their predecessors (give or take thirty centimetres) and only have a single door.

Contract Renewal: Stagecoach Selkent (TL) - 23.1.16
Type Change: ADL Trident/ALX400 to Volvo B5LH/Enviro400 MMC
[13082-13102]

47

In 2006, Catford garage received the very last batch of ALX400 Tridents built for London. 18489-18499 took Stagecoach orders for the type to a round 1,000 and the final batch worked the 47 through two contract periods of ten years. *Above:* 18496 at the start of a southbound journey outside Monument station. After the latest change, the Tridents were divided between Bromley and Barking to replace older vehicles.

You will recall that the first Euro 6 Enviro400 hybrids were tested on the 47 at the start of 2014 before they were used to convert routes 54 and 75.

This batch of twenty-one differ considerably; they have the revamped MMC body and are Volvo-based rather than Dennis, adding to the twenty-one of the same combination delivered to Plumstead in 2015 for a route 177 contract renewal.

Below: 13102 represents the latest group in Tooley Street. You can see more of this batch, at the start of construction, on page 68.

Later in the year, Tooley Street became one-way to accommodate building work (the final phase of the London Bridge station project) and 47s in the southbound direction were diverted along Borough High Street.

ONCE the route 68 conversion finally began, it happened quite quickly. LT667 & 681 appeared first in service, on route 12 on February the 5th, and the others followed within three weeks. There were two absentees from the batch of twenty-four: LT665 was dispatched on a trade mission to Singapore without carrying a single London passenger, and LT684 was mysteriously allocated to Abellio . . . but then not. Day-to-day, up to five or six 'other ranks' continued to appear on the route to make up the shortfall, so it was no great surprise when all the missing numbers – LT684 and 687-90 – were allocated to Camberwell.

Above: LT669 restarts from the Tavistock Square traffic lights. At the back of the queue, LT674 competes for space with the yucky sight-seeing buses.

Opposite page top: The old 68: From a host of possibilities, here's one of Camberwell's Presidents in the Strand. I defy anyone to say with certainty what the type allocation for this route should have been before, other than the rather loose 'red, with wheels at each corner' that pertained day-to-day.
Background notes: The proposal by King's College (background left) to demolish the character buildings (background, right), and

presumably erect another concrete monstrosity, was rejected by Westminster's planning committee in 2014. For once, the mayor did not 'call in' the application and override the council's decision, so you can still enjoy the mix of 19th century architectural styles on your next visit to London . . . unless someone has found a loophole.

Opposite page below: For the first two months of the 68 conversion, a range of other types continued to appear (around five vehicles a day), until the missing LTs made their entrance. From that group, here's LT690 on its first trip, approaching The Old Vic on April 14th.

Fall-Out: Changes to the Camberwell allocation happened almost immediately the 68 conversion began. By the third week of March, many of E164-182 had been stood down (although E163 had mysteriously re-allocated to Merton). All were part of the spare batch transferred to Camberwell after the LT conversion of route 453 at Mandela Way. They would be joined at the end of April by another twenty-nine E400s displaced by the route 345 changeover.

By June, E163-185 had transferred to the new garage at River Road, Barking to service the recently-acquired route 147 (see later). The other former-453 buses (E186-201) remained on Camberwell routes. The group displaced from the 345 (E100-128) were sprayed around various garages, like the Bexleyheath Geminis before them, with the odd one or two going to far-flung locations like Northumberland Park and Silvertown as well as River Road.

Closer to home, three returned to Stockwell and a solitary bus transferred to Sutton to meet a PVR increase on route 213. However, E125 stayed for only a few months before it rejoined the '345 group' in readiness for Merton's takeover of route 57 in July.

To universal surprise, the long-absent LT62 also pitched up to help out. You will recall that this route 11 bus lasted barely a day in service before a disastrous accident in Chelsea Bridge Road in September 2013. After two-and-a half years festering in the Ballymena factory car park, 62 was repaired and resurrected.

By mid-March it was at Bexleyheath, having ETM and iBus re-fitted, and finally reappeared on a London route on April 6th. It lasted a whole two hours before another problem struck and remained out-of-sight for a fortnight before re-emerging on route 12, where it worked almost non-stop for two days (until it ran out of fuel, presumably) and remained fault-free. *Above:* Here it is during a brief pause in its marathon at Oxford Circus on April 22nd.

Right: Lovers of the esoteric will be fascinated to know that LT62 returned to traffic with its platform pole removed, although it retained the inward-opening door. At the same time, I noticed that some of the route 73 buses had received similar treatment – a mixed batch with both inward and sliding leaf doors. I really must get out more (oh, I did, otherwise I wouldn't know this).

Below: The batch became complete on June 21st when LT665 finally went to work on the 68 after its extended holiday in Singapore.

Many of Route 3's new vehicles first appeared on route 159, and for some time afterwards, but the odd one did manage to wind the right number onto its blinds in the early weeks, like LT705 passing The Cenotaph on February 22nd. Mostly, though, the conversion happened with older buses from the 159 batch – LT602-640.

The rogue in the pack was LT704, which worked only nine times between February 15th and March 21st. Once its problems were sorted, it became super-reliable, as is often the way after a difficult start.

Below: For the last contract renewal in February 2012, Abellio ordered a batch of Enviro400 hybrids, 2414-37. Later they became mixed with deliveries of similar vehicles for routes 49, 211 and C3, but this is one of the originals – 2426 – on the south side of Lambeth Bridge. The bus still looks remarkably smart, despite four years of hacking around south London. I used to go to school on the 3 . . . you know.

Above: Two days after entering service (on the 3, surprisingly), LT710 has gravitated towards the 159 and is passing the revised pavement layout at Kennington Park.

The cycleway improvements at this location and others have divided opinion – a great environmental step forward to some, a jam-creating nightmare to others. I take a different view; all these extra paving enclosures provide convenient new spots for photographers . . . although spending a hundred million quid on us seems a bit excessive.

Fall-Out: *Battersea allocation changes*
The Enviro400 hybrids ordered for route 3's 2012 contract renewal transferred to Walworth and appeared immediately on routes 35,

40, 188 & 381. This was one of the batches ordered by Abellio with National Express-style interiors (grey moquette, red poles) to match the other Enviros at Battersea. The later scheme (dark red moquette, yellow poles) was expected to replace the original design when the batch was refurbished. The status of a fire-damaged 2429 was resolved in May when it re-entered service from Walworth..

The influx of newer kit spelled the end for some of the Tridents in the 98XX series bought second-hand in 2011 for a route 172 contract renewal – a truly horrible batch whose interiors looked like someone's child had sneezed violently in a finger-painting class.

A handful of original Tridents (97XX series, ordered by Travel London) remained at Battersea for a short time on route C3.

Contract Renewals with 'existing fleet'
in the January/February period

Route 184 E20D 9.6m/Enviro200	Arriva LN (WN) – 6.2.16 [PVR 20]	**Route B12** E200 Dart/Enviro200	Arriva KT (DT) – 23.1.16 [PVR 7]
Route 263 ADL Trident/Enviro400	Metroline (PB) – 6.2.16 [PVR 18]	**Route W5** Optare Solo M880	CT Plus (HK) – 6.2.16 [PVR 8]
		Route W10 Dart SLF/Capital	London General (NP) – 6.2.16 [PVR 1]

Above: From the vast collection of 10.2 metre E200 Darts, this is ENL32 passing Barnet Church soon after starting a southbound journey on route 184 in 2014. The allocation returned to Wood Green garage in November of that year after a brief sojourn at Edmonton. A solitary double-decker continued to appear in the morning and evening peaks as the contract was renewed.

Below: I kept expecting something interesting to happen at Potters Bar, but the long-term pattern of more-or-less common-user E400s continued on the 82 and 263, with rather more of the newer batch on the central London route. Ergo, here is a perfectly ordinary TE950 from the correct batch on the 263 at Archway in 2011 – a scene repeated in 2012, 13, 14, 15 & 16 but not necessarily with the blue skirt.

Opposite page: The ever-present DMN1, doyen of route W10. However, it will be almost fifteen years old by the time you first read this. Very few vehicles last that long in London, so expect the clock to run down finally in 2017.

LT CONVERSION
Metroline (HT) – 6.2.16
Type Change: ADL Trident/Enviro400
to Wright New Routemaster
[LT745-766 & ST812]

91

THE old 91 had been worked by London's very first batch of Enviro400s since the start of 2006, but Metroline's cranky numbering system disguised their pedigree. *Below:* From that batch, TE665-692, this is a refurbished TE666 at Aldwych in 2013. On the left is Harrod's electric delivery van 952, built somewhere around 1939 and still running in restored form in the summer months.

Above: Mid-way through the conversion, LT751 descends Crouch End Hill and meets TE681 on the way up.

The 91's former Enviros remained at Holloway, spread around routes 4, 17, 43 and 271, allowing a number of freed-up VWs to transfer to Brentford for the double-decking of route E8 (see May/June section).

ST812

After conducting road tests over several routes pencilled in for LT conversion, TfL identified the need for a shorter bus – not least to negotiate mini-roundabouts along the journey. On at least two – the C2 and the 91 – the problem occurred at the start of the London-bound trip, where it proved impossible to turn the 11.3 metre vehicles with any degree of accuracy, never mind repeatability. At only 10.2 metres, ST2001 was meant to be the solution, but the plan was rather overtaken by events.

After a lengthy delay, the short bus appeared as ST812 for the route 91 conversion in May but, by then, the incoming mayor had already made his "no more LTs" announcement. The only other possibility was that some of the remaining build (LT813-1000) would be to the shorter length for restricted routes, although the recently-announced SRM (a 10.6m body on a Volvo chassis – see elsewhere) was clearly the better solution. *Below:* Internally, the length reduction resulted in the loss of a seating bay. Externally, apart from a suspicion of stubbiness, it's doubtful whether the 91's travellers noticed any difference between 812 and the rest of the new buses.

Left: And here's the root of the problem – the roundabout at Crouch End where the 91s turn at the start of the southbound journey. Although the remodelling was completed before the first NRM entered service, it remained a tight fit. LT757 is on full lock but there are only inches to spare.

Quite Interesting 1

RATHER than devote another full page to route 91, I've put this first picture in Quite Interesting because it's . . . erm, quite interesting.

It has become commonplace for garages to run brand-new LTs for a newly-converted route on an earlier one, but Holloway resisted the temptation until almost half the 91s were in service. *Above:* LT762 breaks the mould with a first day appearance on the 390 on May 21st. This is the Notting Hill Gate stand outside the Post Office. As later vehicles with a sliding rear door and no pole could not be 'second-manned', such substitutions only happened at weekends on the 390 and not at all on the 24. Then, of course, all the so-called customer assistants were directed to the nearest Job Centre and the distinction became academic.

Below: After I reported the last Plaxton President on Stockwell's allocation in the 2015 *RAO*, five more transferred there barely four days after the book was printed – more fall-out from the hybrid invasion of Merton garage. At first the PVLs kept to route 249 with makeshift blinds, but became fully common-user when the complete set turned up on a roll. Here, for instance, is PVL379 on route 87, rounding the giant pineapple on the north side of Lambeth Bridge. The first five had become nine by the middle of March, prompting the question:
Why put Euro-3 buses back on the 87 after the route had been 'cleaned up' with hybrids displaced from the 88?
Answer: Because they were really at Stockwell to take over the 249 when that route's Volvos transferred to east London (read on).

Above: The scattering of redundant Volvo B9s within Go-Ahead has happened before – for example, when route 12 converted to LTs in 2015. One of the batch had already been travelling, however; WVL450 was loaned to Stockwell in September 2013 and, barely a fortnight later, suffered a major accident that kept it off the road for ten months. The bus clocked up another fortnight at Stockwell after repair, but then returned to Camberwell before something else untoward happened to it.

The route 12 conversion prompted another move, this time north of the river. As a Northumberland Park bus, WVL450 has mainly been confined to the 191, but sometimes works into central London on either the 259 or 476. When photographed at Euston in February 2016, it was still carrying the SW garage codes applied when it returned to Stockwell two years earlier. Because it's worked far fewer journeys than others in its batch, the interior looks almost like new.

Below: Staying with the 'coming back after a long period away' theme, here's LT1 outside Simpson of Piccadilly after its return to route 38 as LTZ1001 in 2016. There was a concerted effort to get the missing prototypes back on the road in the new year, and this eventually culminated in all eight working on the same day – 1-7 on the 38 and LT8 on the 390 on March the 8th. I doubt this had ever happened before; even when the last two prototypes arrived in the late summer of 2012, it was rare to find more than three or four on the 38 at any one time.

By November LT1 was off the road and, soon after, set off on its travels through the Americas. The best performance after that was in April 2013, when the remaining seven appeared in the course of a single day.

River Road Garage Barking

Changes to East London Transit came into effect on March 19th with the re-routing of EL2 from Barking station to Becontree – largely to relieve overcrowding on route 5. *Opposite page top:* Three of the dedicated vehicles – WVL338, 451 & 341 – grace the patch of concrete known as Becontree Heath bus station. The middle bus is one of four transferred from Camberwell in the route 12 clear-out. They first went to Silvertown before transferring to Rainham to boost the ELTs.

Opposite Centre: The latest change called for a combined PVR increase of twelve, which was met by the transfer of route 249's Volvo B9s from Stockwell (WVL468-480). Here's two of the Stockwell vehicles at the Alderman Way stop near the southern end of the 'system'. WVL477 is working as EL2, WVL471 as EL1. Previously, both routes covered the same ground from here to Ilford station and part of the PVR increase was to maintain the former frequency between Barking and Ilford now that EL1 was working the section alone. Day-to-day, all three batches (totalling thirty-three buses) mixed and mingled at random.

Readers with long memories will recall this began as a proposal for a tramway system when Ken Livingstone was London mayor. The idea was later down-graded to hybrid buses, then diesel buses.

Opposite Below: By July, the Stockwell imports had been adorned with the regular ELT vinyls, like WVL470 approaching the Barking station stop. Then came the announcement that EL1, EL2 and the soon-to-be-created EL3 would convert to NRMs in February 2017. Some people are still reeling from the shock. By the way, I took all of these on different days, so refer to the picture above for confirmation that the sun does shine in Barking sometimes.

Above: The new garage in River Road is only a short hop from the EL1 & EL2's line of route. The whole fleet went west at the start of July when Rainham closed; the new facility also took in the recently-acquired 147. For a while, it resided there in splendid isolation. *Photo: Ken Carr*

Below: Both batches of Ash Grove's Enviro400s made their way further east to upgrade Arriva Barking routes. Here, for instance, is a refurbished T170 during a crew change at the Althorne Way stop in March while working the 128. When new in 2010, this was one of a batch dedicated to route 168 and therefore a regular at Waterloo and Euston. Althorne Way is now the first stop of the southbound EL2 after leaving the bus station. It's also served by refurbished Enviros on the 150.

London United's contract for the 94 had been extended by two years from 17th October 2015 under the Quality Incentive scheme, so a partial upgrading of the route with more hybrids looked like a pre-emptive strike before the re-tendering process in 2017.

There were fourteen new Geminis eventually – VH45153-66 – and their appearance eliminated diesel Tridents (TLAs) from the route. The earlier Enviro400 hybrids (ADH3-22) remained; so, more to the point, the much-debated Noxford Street moved ever closer to full hybrid operation. The exceptions, for the moment, were a handful of diesel Enviros and early Geminis on the 23 and the Presidents of the 98.

Top: In its first week, VH45153 pauses at Lancaster Gate with one of the originals close behind. This bus would have been VH53 (carrying on from the route 116 series) but for RATP's renumbering of its entire London fleet.

Above: Name that font: It's obviously not the TfL-approved Johnston, nor is it Helvetica, Arial, Geneva or Verdana because the 'ones' have serifs, but neither is it Palatino nor Times Roman. That's all the popular fonts accounted for, so this must be a new RATP design. Is it Parisian, perhaps?

Right: A revised seat moquette also appeared on the new intake – a return to the dowdy after the striking and attractive multi-coloured circles first applied to London United vehicles in 2012.

The saga resurfaces later in the book under route 72, although route 85 is next upgrade-wise.

Top: The early DW type (DAF DB250s) continued on the endangered list in 2016, although withdrawals halted temporarily in the first half of the year. The handful transferred to Enfield in 2015 were joined by a few more at the start of the new year. This is DW32 at Turnpike Lane in April.

By the autumn, none remained on Enfield routes but some of the lower numbers were still working in north London, on Overground replacement route T between Walthamstow and Barking (see pp 28/29). South Croydon retained around thirty DB250s for front-line work and there were half-a-dozen 'Shires' survivors, renumbered as Arriva London North DWs and operating out of Garston.

Centre: Gemini 2DLs were commonplace on this stretch of tarmac before the 159 converted to LTs. After only a few months, the type was back at Marble Arch, this time running from Norwood on route 2. DW278 was one of several in a similar number series displaced from Brixton, but their outings on the 2 became sporadic after the contract renewal of the 417 in August – the route for which the refurbs were intended.

Left: Many of the DB250 Geminis at South Croydon were superseded by DB300 Gemini 2DLs, displaced from north London routes by LTs. One of the transfers, DW268, clocked up more than a year of almost daily service before suffering a major accident involving a tree in the small hours of November 7th (2015). The Enfield repair centre showed its usual expertise with the rebuild but the bus didn't reappear until 20th June – repainted but not fully refurbished. Here it is, looking very shiny, on route 264's stand in Katharine Street, Croydon.

Above: Although there are daily call-outs to engineers to attend to minor problems, total failures at the roadside remain rare. On this occasion, VW1865 has failed to respond and a Sovereign truck is needed to tow it back to Willesden.

Below: So there I was, tucking into a cheese sandwich, when this appeared without warning – BYD double-decker number 2 on test over route 98. I was immediately reminded of trips to the circus as a young sprog, and the clown's car whose doors and wheels flew off in a cloud of smoke. Maybe there should be fewer brightly-coloured stickers next time.

Above: The Battersea Power Station workers' shuttles continued in 2016 and are likely to do so for a considerable time. Various Go-Ahead vehicles have provided the service since it began, mostly spare Presidents. The last time I saw PVL219, for instance, it was conveying rich people to the Chelsea Flower Show as a front-line member of the Commercial Services fleet. The bus has just dropped off a full load of workpersons at Vauxhall interchange before returning to the site to collect more. Although the upgrade of the Underground station's booking hall was in full swing, the blue hoardings in the background were surrounding only grass and fresh air. Baffling.

The unique DW411 eventually became super-reliable on Enfield routes for much of 2015, but vanished off the radar again in January 2016. It reappeared in June, with a number of lengthy tests on route 121, and then became a daily regular again on the 349.

Below: The StreetDeck test bed moves off from Seven Sisters station. Meanwhile, another member of the test trio, SW1, had moved north from Wood Green to Garston to familiarise engineering staff with the mechanicals before the introduction of StreetDeck look-alikes on route 340 in August (see later).

Gospel Oak-Barking ... by bus

WHEN I was a full-time railway aficionado, Gospel Oak was a strange backwater we scooted past on railtours, its only point of interest an ancient DMU churning away in a separate platform. That, I discovered later, was the departure point for self-contained services to Barking which, in the modern world, were absorbed into the London Overground network.

However, owing to the lack of electrons thereon, a fleet of eight diesel-powered Turbostars had operated the section since 2010. Before that, it was Sprinters (lovely).

All that will now change, with the erection of catenary and an order for 25kV Ventura units, but the work has demanded a partial closure of the line since June 2016 and a complete closure since September.

The replacement bus service has operated in two sections - from Gospel Oak-Seven Sisters (Service J) and Walthamstow-Barking (Service T). An eclectic mix of former-and existing front-line buses has been deployed and, at weekends, New Routemasters from Arriva garages.

Travellers wishing to make the full journey on the Go-Bark have had to use both bus routes and the Victoria Line as a connection between Seven Sisters and Walthamstow - a tortuous trip, to put it mildly. They will also have discovered that the station 'calling points' were not necessarily where they expected to find them.

For the full history of the line, consult Wikipedia. For fun, dial up HISTORY LO-T on LVF and marvel at the huge list of bus types that have appeared on the main route. You will also find there are six pages of LTs.

Opposite page top: At the eastern extremity of Route T, DW75 will shortly go back to Walthamstow from Barking station after turning at the Longford Road roundabout. In the background, the Spotted Dog and, further along, the Barking Dog (naturally).

The bus (which is what you're interested in, not the pubs), transferred from Brixton garage in January 2015 and spent more than a year on Garston routes in the Far North. It moved to the T (or UL7) in June 2016 and was still working it almost every day in December.

Opposite Below: At the other end, VLA162 sets off from Walthamstow Central. This is another Brixton bus, but withdrawn in January 2016. After five months out of use, it also joined the T pool in June.

And now the first head scratch: On the day I decided to take some pictures, I stupidly went to Gospel Oak station, only to be told: "No, mate, no buses 'ere." After reading 'Stop GN Gordon House Road' in the publicity bumph, and tracing stop GN Gordon House Road on TfL route maps, I found the starting point . . . in Highgate Road.

Above: Metroline's VP510 waits time at the stop. There were three of us on this bus all the way to Finsbury Park. I also discovered that the Crouch Hill set-down was nowhere near Crouch Hill station but on a completely different railway bridge. According to the same publicity, it was "800 metres - please walk or use local bus 210".

Route T's oddity was Leytonstone High Road station, whose set-down was at Harrow Green, three bus stops away.

If you're the adventurous type, this interesting experience will be available until February . . . or when the work is finished.

AFTER a quiet few weeks in March, April exploded in a frenzy of activity with thirteen contract renewals on a single day, many with new vehicles. There was also a sudden influx of MMC single-deckers after a slow start for the type and the reappearance of some of the discarded StreetLites delivered new to London General in 2014 for route 192. There was also this . . .

LT CONVERSION
Arriva LS (BN) – 2.4.16
Type Change: DB300 & Volvo B5LH/ Gemini to Wright New Routemaster [LT716-744]

59

ANOTHER long-rumoured conversion began in a great rush on 22nd March when ten vehicles appeared on the 59 in a single day – unusual for a cascade changeover rather than a contract change.

Opposite: The first of the batch may have appeared on the 137 the night before, so to cover that base (if it happened), here's LT719 at Hyde Park Corner station on the 23rd.

After the initial swathe, no new buses appeared for almost a fortnight and the only notable working in that time was LT723's appearance, with other Arriva LTs, on the Highbury to Shadwell Overground replacements. The section was shut for ten days but NRMs only appeared at weekends. The 'spread' of new vehicles onto the 59 lasted for about five weeks until the final bus, LT740, appeared on April 28th.

Top & Above: Swops with buses from the earlier batch at Brixton continued, and several others made their first journeys on the 137.

For the sake of authenticity, however, here's a brand-new LT733 working the correct route at Tenison Way. At the same time, buses in the LT3XX number series often appeared on the 59, so we have LT338 promoting the power of plants in Upper Woburn Place. Fans of Prezzo will be relieved to hear that the Euston branch and the building above emerged unscathed from the white plastic by the autumn.

Main Picture, top left: Those of you who remember Brixton garage when it was full of original Routemasters may be slightly shocked by the 2016 view, but the world moves on. For the advert spotters again, the two full-wrap buses are LT338 (Crunchie) and LT328 (Mr Burberry Fragrance).

At the back of the hive, it is just possible to glimpse the odd Gemini. The B5 hybrids were now working the 319, the remaining 2DLs were assigned to route 50. Later in the year, Brixton became 100% hybrid when HVs displaced from Stamford Hill replaced the diesel DWs.

THREE routes crossed from one side of Camberwell New Road to the other on April 30th when the 35 and 40 contracts (combined PVR 40) were taken over by Go-Ahead's Camberwell garage and the 345 (PVR25) transferred to Abellio Walworth. It may safely be assumed that Fall-Out ensued because of a) the number of new buses ordered, and b) the lower vehicle requirement created at Walworth. Read on.

Contract Change: Abellio (WL) to London Central (Q) – 30.4.16
Type Change: Trident/Enviro400 to ADL E40H/Enviro400 MMC [EH39-60]

35

Walworth garage (strictly speaking, Walworth depot, as it's Abellio) had a common-user pool of diesel E400s which appeared mostly but not exclusively on the 35 and 40. Both routes also produced Volvo B7/Geminis normally found on the 188. *Opposite page top:* 9462, entering the Brixton one-way system, is from a batch of thirty-nine Enviros (9428-66) delivered for the last contract renewal of the 35 in 2009 (five years plus two).

Opposite page: Although MMCs were ordered for route 35 and EvoSetis for route 40, the whole lot operated as a brand-new common-user pool from the first morning . . . but EH57 is on the correct route (if you're obsessed with such things) at the Rookery Road stop on Clapham Common. Heading in the opposite direction on the 345 is 2418, one of Walworth's allocation of E400 hybrids, which itself worked the 35 only two days earlier. This is a lovely spot for photography when the sun is in the right position, but you will have to cope with lots of traffic and lots of joggers.

Top: Crew change time at Camberwell Green. The start of the afternoon shift produces a collection of new kit only a few hundred yards from the garage. EH39 & 53 and MHV18 are allocated to the 35; EH47 sets off southwards with a new driver on the 40. The two routes shadow each other from here to Fenchurch Street, running via Elephant & Castle and London Bridge.
Left: EH51 & EH45 at the Shoreditch stand on the first day.

THE other half of the 35/40 swop produced a new type combination on London's streets – the MCV Evoseti body, built in Egypt, on the well-established Volvo B5L hybrid chassis. The 'old' 40 was also worked by a common-user pool at Walworth, so earlier comments apply. Here's a selection of pics taken at the Belvedere compound two days before the new vehicles entered service.

Contract Change: Abellio (WL) to London Central (Q) – 30.4.16
Type Change: Trident/Enviro400 to Volvo B5LH/MCV EvoSeti [MHV1-20]

40

Above: The lower deck of EvoSeti MHV8, showing MCV's corner 'build-around' that the B5LH chassis requires. The reason for it becomes clear in the Volvo article on page 68.

FUEL

DIESEL

Adblue

FUEL ID CODE 9659

VOLVO

MHV9

Go Ahead-London
LONDON CENTRAL

SCREEN WASH

eVoSeti

MHV8

HYBRID
CLEANERAIR
FOR LONDON

Above & Left: Exterior detail of MHV8 & 9.

Below: A general view of Belvedere on 28th April. As you may guess, all of Camberwell's double-deck numbers are on the blinds.

The main picture *(opposite top)* shows the new common-user pool at full throttle: EH45, 51 & 50 (ordered for route 35) at route 40's 'temporary' stand in Houndsditch. Although Aldgate bus station re-opened on 5th May, buses arriving from the Fenchurch Street direction were no longer allowed to turn right into Minories as the road had become two-way in the re-modelling. The 40s therefore continued to use the stand where they'd been since the work began. Their first stop remained St Botolph Street, followed by Aldgate High Street (just before the bus station exit).

45

EH60

Ahead-London
LONDON CENTRAL

16 OCS

MHV9

BU16 OYS

Camberwell Green 468

EH50

YX16 OCF

Aldwych 68

Go

BU16 OZ

Contract Change: London Central (Q) to Abellio (WL) – 30.4.16
Vehicle Change: Trident/Enviro400 to Enviro400 various
(but mostly ex-35 & 40)

345

Route 345's last contract renewal in 2009 generated a batch of new Enviro400s, E100-128, originally allocated to Stockwell (London General). All were delivered in June/July of that year, but transferred to Camberwell (London Central) in 2012 to make room for even more new vehicles when Go-Ahead won the route 19 contract from Arriva. Although they remained constant performers on the 345, a common-user approach ensured they appeared daily on Camberwell's other routes as well.
Above: The regular view of the old 345 – E118, in full Go-Ahead livery, pulling away from the Stockwell station stop as Q514.

Abellio put out a mixture of ADL types on the first day – half hybrids, half refurbished diesels. First out was 2415 at 00:42 on the night route.
Below: Within a week or so, Walworth's allocation of MMC Enviros

(ordered for routes 415 & 432) began to appear in ones and twos. Here's 2516 restarting after the Cedars Road stop in uptown Clapham.

Fall-Out: The next chapter for the 345's Go-Ahead Enviros unfolds later in the book as a neatly satisfying full batch changeover. The Abellio changes are slightly harder to pin down; many of the last day runners on the 35, for instance, moved straight to the 345 and other routes at Walworth (all were E400 variants). Two transferred to Battersea, and the higher-numbered diesels, 9460-5, moved to Hayes for the E9 when Abellio took over the route in May.

By contrast, every one of route 40's last day runners remained at Walworth, although the Volvo B7/Geminis were thereafter confined to routes 188/343/381.

The 28's renewal involved a partial upgrade from one type of Volvo to another. *Above:* The old is represented by one of the huge collection of Geminis inherited by Tower Transit at Westbourne Park and Atlas Road. Most were the 10.1 metre variant, like VNW32374 passing the trendy shops of Notting Hill pre-Tower in 2013.

The replacements were Volvo B9/Eclipse Geminis from a small batch for route 295, introduced in September 2012 but displaced by Gemini 3 hybrids towards the end of 2015 when that contract changed hands. Because of this early availability, the upgrade of the 28 happened much

Contract Renewal: Tower Transit (AS) – 30.4.16
Partial Type Change: Volvo B7 to Volvo B9/Eclipse Gemini (VN37988-96 ex-295)

28

sooner than the 30th April contract date. Needless to say, there was overlap with similar vehicles delivered to Westbourne Park/Atlas Road for routes 23 and 266. *Below:* VN37993, from the former-295 batch, is about to turn into Palace Gardens Terrace while heading south.

Contract Renewal: Tower Transit (AS) – 30.4.16
Type Change: Volvo B7TL/Eclipse Gemini to Volvo B5LH/Gemini 3
[VH38112-38136]

328

Above: Tower's common-user pool of 10.1 metre Geminis also serviced routes 31 and 328, so here's VNW32364 at the World's End stand before setting off on the long drag to Golders Green. With a 6-7 minute frequency over its eight miles, the route has a substantial PVR of 28.

Below: Mid-way through the changeover from Gemini 1 to 3, VH38124 passes St Philip's Church in Earl's Court Road. In the background 38115 heads north after emerging from the one-way system on either side of

Cromwell Road. The replacement buses began to appear from 21st March, almost six weeks ahead of the contract date.

After various combinations during the transition to full-blown Gemini 3, all vehicles delivered to London operators in 2016 had the restyled front and back panels of the StreetDeck, but not the glass-framed stairs on the off-side. You will also note that the addition of an upper case qualifier on the destination blind was not confined to the LT fleet.

If route 62 rings a bell and you can't think why, maybe it's because the last London RTs worked on the route in 1979 (assuming you were hatched by then). In the present day, 'various' in the context of the old contract means Tridents of both kinds, Optare Versas and Enviro200s (pretty much anything on Barking's allocation is another description).
Above: Here, for instance, is 19801 at Barking station, although single-deckers were the closest thing to 'a norm'.

Below: Transition in the garage yard - 10331 entered service on route 62 on 14th April, but common-user allocation soon became apparent. On this

Contract Renewal: **Stagecoach EL (BK) – 30.4.16**
Type Change: **Various to E40D/Enviro400 MMC [from 10308-332]**

62

particular day, for instance, there were more new vehicles on the 387; on others, they were all on the 145. The last of the batch of twenty-five appeared on 24th May (10311 on route 5).

Contract Renewal: Stagecoach EL (BK) – 30.4.16
Type Change: Trident/Enviro400
to E40D/Enviro400 MMC
[from 10308-332]

145

Routes 145 and 294 follow the 62 because all three were upgraded with one, large batch of Enviro400 diesel MMCs. Before the change, route 145 was predominately worked by various E400s backed up by the classic Trident/ ALX400 combination. *Above:* 19798 turns at Faircross, outside the home garage, while on its way to Leytonstone. Barking had more than sixty Euro-4 Enviros on its books from Stagecoach London's massive orders for the type in 2011/12.

Meanwhile, a few miles further east, a continuation of the batch went to North Street for the conversion of route 294, spelling the end for yet more Tridents. *Below:* Apart from the mad clutter of modern street furniture and some tinkering with the pavement, this view of the Harold Wood station stop has hardly changed in fifty years. Trident 17986 calls in on its way to Havering Park in 2015.

Contract Renewal: Stagecoach EL (NS) – 30.4.16
Type Change: Trident/ALX400
to E40D/Enviro400 MMC
[10333-347]

294

Rounding off the Barking area changes on 30th April, route 368 not only changed operater but double-decked itself to boot. Since 2013, Rainham garage had maintained a fleet of eight E200s inherited from First Capital when it took over the routes of the Dagenham Chequers Lane operation. SEN30-7 started life as DMV44271-8. They were new at the last contract renewal in 2011 so obviously retained their First Group interior trim. All eight appeared on the final day. *Above:* SEN35 in Barking Town Centre earlier in the week. As a bonus, you get another E200 on the 62.

The Ash Grove Enviros mentioned earlier also featured in the 368's conversion. By the first week of May, two batches – T65-83 & 168-193 – were forming a common user pool at Arriva Barking for routes 128, 150, 173 (another single-deck upgrade) and the 368, although a number of VLAs continued to appear on the 128. *Below:* A hot summer day enhances a shiny T80 at the Longford Road roundabout. The shop in the background confirms the weather forecast.

Contract Change: Blue Triangle (BE) to Arriva LN (DX) – 30.4.16
Type Change: E20D/Enviro200 to Trident/Enviro400
[existing fleet]

368

Route 69 was created from trolleybus 669 in 1960 with new RMs from Walthamstow garage and, later, Leyton. It was worked throughout the privatised era by Stagecoach East London, so the transfer of the contract to Tower before the official date of 30th April raised eyebrows on both counts. Until Enviro400s became available from Tower's loss of route 26 at the end of June, the company hired in the existing Stagecoach Tridents. 18237-256 were backed up by the occasional Enviro from the 26/30 pool.

Above: 'Old' 69 – one of West Ham's huge collection of Tridents at Stratford Broadway in 2013. 150 years after his death, the weighty memorial to local philanthropist Samuel Gurney continues to

dominate the scene. On this side of Stratford, very little has changed in recent decades and it's hard to believe the London Olympics took place barely a mile away.

Until the full batch of Enviro400s came 'off loan' to CT Plus, Tower filled in with whatever came to hand. When the hired Stagecoach Tridents went back, for instance, E400s normally found on route 425 substituted as required, like DN33778 below. E400s borrowed from route 30 were replaced by Geminis normally found on other Tower routes in east London. Readers will recall that this game of musical buses ensued when Tower began operating the Virtual Electric E400s on the 69 (see the 2015 *RAO*), prompting the change of contract date.

Contract Change: Stagecoach EL (BK) to CT Plus (HK) – 30.4.16
Type Change: Trident/ALX400 to E40D/Enviro400
[from DN33612-655]

69

Contract Renewal: London General (MB) – 19.3.16
Partial Vehicle Change: E20D/Enviro200 to similar
[SE288-90]

162

Go-Ahead ordered three Enviros to the 'classic pattern' for the route 162 renewal but they were immediately put to work on another Orpington route, the 138. Thereafter, their appearances on the 162 were no more or less frequent than on others as members of the common-user pool.

Above: One photo, then, illustrates both the old contract and the new: 173, another 8.9 metre Enviro200, arrives at the St George's Church stop in Beckenham. After the final trio of old-style E200s for the 162, it was MMCs all the way in London . . . until CT Plus unexpectedly resurrected the classic design.

Below: The Esteems formerly on route 367 (in the range 257-266) were only ten years old, but all were stood down after the contract passed to Abellio. The new MMCs kicked off a mini-avalanche of the type in the ensuing months. At 8995 mm, the short version would perhaps be nine metres in a strong wind, but ADL continues to describe this variant as 8.9m in its literature.

Abellio ordered ten to service a PVR of 9 and this is 8218 restarting from East Croydon bus station. Like earlier Enviro200s, the single-door model has an off-side emergency exit. The new buses are powered by 4.5 litre Euro-6 Cummins units, but larger engines are available.

Contract Change: London General (C) to Abellio (BC) – 19.3.16
Type Change: Dart SLF/East Lancs Esteem to E20D/Enviro200 MMC
[8210-19]

367

Quality Line took ten vehicles in the range WS33-48 and renumbered them as WS01-10 for the route 463 upgrade. On-loan StreetLite demonstrator SN65 OKM, renumbered WS11, also appeared on the route in 2016, still with London United branding.

The 64-reg buses were originally with Go-Ahead – part of the 16-strong group that first converted route 192 in 2014/15. They went off-lease when flywheel-fitted replacements turned up six months later, but were re-leased to Epsom garage for the 463. *Above:* WS09 (G-A's WS47) completes a southbound journey at Coulsdon South station.

The bridge in the background carries the Brighton main line via Quarry Tunnel, whereas Coulsdon South is on the original line via Redhill (look it up in your Rail Atlas).

Metroline ordered a dozen MMCs for the route 487 renewal but they remained invisible for three months after the contract date. When they did materialise in June, they went into store at Perivale amid reports that changes to infrastructure were needed to accommodate their extra length. Eventually they went to work in ones and twos on Uxbridge garage routes in the 'U' series, but there was still one missing by the end of the year.

Below: DE1600 arrives at South Harrow station. This is from a huge batch of 10.2 metre Dart/Enviros ordered by First Centrewest in 2008/9 and originally numbered DML44007-44128.

Contract Renewal: Metroline West (ON) – 5.3.16
Type Change: E200 Dart 10.2m/Enviro200 to
E20D 10.8m/Enviro200 MMC [DEL2155-66]

487

Contract Renewal: Abellio (QB/WL) – 19.3.16
Type Change: E200 Dart 10.2m/Enviro200 to
E20D 10.8m/Enviro200 MMC
[8844-8864]

C10

Adding to the extensive single-deck action in March, we have Abellio's upgrade of the C10 from one kind of Enviro200 to another.
Above: 8562, one of a large number of 10.2 metre Darts based in south London, was photographed outside The Westminster in 2011. Since then, the pub has been demolished and something with less character has risen in its place. ADL's literature (referred to earlier) describes the longer vehicles in the replacement batch as 10.8 metre (10870mm).

Go-Ahead's tentative first order for E200 MMCs continued numerically from the Orpington trio mentioned two pages back. However, these are described as 9.7 metre – a third length to get our heads around.
Below: As all MMCs look the same from a distance (sorry, ADL, but they do), here's one of the older vehicles on the route, decked out in full Go-Ahead bling. SE88 emerges from Coldharbour Lane and begins the one-way circuit in front of Lambeth Town Hall.

Contract Renewal: London Central (Q) – 30.4.16
Partial Type Change: Various s/d to
E20D 9.7m/Enviro200 MMC   [SE291-2]

P5

Contract Renewals with 'existing fleet'
in the March/April period

Route 187	Metroline West (W) - 5.3.16	**Route 484**	Abellio (WL) - 19.3.16
E200 Dart/Enviro200	PVR 15	E200 Dart 9.3m/Enviro200	PVR 9
Route 315	London General (SW) - 30.4.16	**Route H32**	London United (AV) - 5.3.16
Dart SLF/Pointer	PVR 4	Scania OmniCity	PVR 13
Route 366	Stagecoach EL (BK) - 30.4.16	**Route H91**	London United (HH) - 5.3.16
E20D 10.2m/Enviro200	PVR 18	Scania OmniCity	PVR 14

Top: Route 315's Dart Pointers reached their tenth birthday in 2016, so their inclusion becomes more relevant. This is LDP289 approaching the junction of Garrad's Road with Tooting Bec Road in Streatham – not far from the St Leonard's Church stop. By the autumn there were still around sixty LDPs working for Go-Ahead on both sides of the river, although most were in the south. Withdrawals will continue as new vehicles, like the Red Arrow electrics, create cascades through the fleet.

Above: Identical to each other in almost every respect, 8327 & 8338 wait between journeys at the former bus park in front of Lewisham station. Both were delivered on the cusp of UK conformance Darts giving way to EC type approval E20Ds – a time when some of the old spec appeared with the headlight slots meant to indicate the new spec. It only happened on single-deckers, not E400s, so this photo might be considered by some as historically important . . . or it might not.

Opposite: Here's a blast from the past – a centre staircase President on the H32 in Hanworth Road, Hounslow. In 2016 the oldest bus you were likely to find on the route was an ALX400/Trident alongside more modern kit like the Enviro400 and Scania OmniCity. Note also the gardening effort, barely a metre from such a busy main road.

Opposite top: Not a million miles away, H91's contract was renewed on the same date. Before their transfer to Stamford Brook, the first two Enviro400 hybrids were frequent performers on the route, so here's ADH2 completing another journey at a sun-drenched Hounslow West.

Vinyl Variations 1

THE change of emphasis first noticed in 2015 continued as more and more all-over wraps migrated to the LT fleet rather than appearing on regular buses. In fact, it would be fair to say that the NRMs became London's official moving hoardings as the year unfolded. There was such a vast selection that they've been split into two parts again.

The January-June period kicks off with the explosion of Sky Q vinyls, known officially as 'red' and 'blue'. I don't begin to understand Sky packages, although I have heard people raving about 'cubes'.

Above: LT50 runs around Aldwych, showing off the full red design. Some of you may actually know what those blobs represent. The same bus resurfaced in the autumn with a more traditional appearance (see part two).

Below: Although red fronts have been the norm on wrapped regular buses, I can't recall seeing an LT in this guise. LT570's 'partial' is the result of an accident repair and repaint in May. The bus was missing for about four weeks, during which time some of the original vinyl disappeared.

Above: On the regular bus front (strictly speaking, regular bus back and sides), Route 23's hybrids continued their long association with holiday destinations – hence DNH39117 promoting Taiwan at Marble Arch in April. By the time this book is published, the tower block in the right background will have vanished in the Odeon Cinema redevelopment project.

Left: The main fleet's tentative hold on vinyl continued to be boosted by a multitude of back wraps. VW1398 is promoting the discounted one-journey fare available with contactless payment and Oyster. The comparison with a stamp is rather clever; most people think postage rates are outrageous, therefore £1.50 for a bus ride of maybe eight miles must be good value.

Below: Meanwhile, back at the LTs, there were lots of these wasp-like concoctions buzzing around in the spring to promote L'Oreal's Studio Pro range. The design was meant to represent a 35mm film strip, but the whole thing just looked a mess to me. One of the Stockwell pool rumbles along Whitehall while on route 88 duty. Later in the year, LT68 was promoting Spotify.

Above & Right: After making the poor bloke appear in his pants in 2015, Tommy Hilfiger allowed Rafa Nadal to play tennis in one of its suits for the Mark 3 version advert. The different designs on opposite sides also went for the film strip approach but without the clumsy black surrounds.

This is LT704 at the Marble Arch stand of route 159. I have formed the theory that you can photograph every single all-over wrap if you stand at this location for long enough.

Below: See what I mean? LT95 motors past the spring planting while promoting the Pizza Express Hawaiian – a startling but short-lived design which left no doubt that the Hawaiian is the one with the pineapple.

Above: Viva Glam's pink design featured a line of scantily-clad eye candy – a device often resorted to by advertisers. What did it all mean? No-one cared. LT720 in the glamorous surroundings of Clapham Common.

Left: This eye-catching cartoon celebrated the fiftieth anniversary of Vans shoes, an American product to be worn only by the seriously trendy. LT476 at Oxford Circus. I have formed the theory that you can photograph every single all-over wrap if you stand at this location for long enough.

Below: Here's a new twist – vodka from America. This imported spirit, distilled in California, is said to be smooth enough to drink straight. Good luck with that. LT145 at the Palace Gardens Terrace stop. There are some who still believe this to have been a holiday ad.

Above: Burberry is best-known for its robust outerwear, but here we have the Mr Burberry fragrance for the more sensitive chap, promoted by a young Richard Hammond. LT605 waits time at . . . oh, it's Marble Arch again.

Right: Meanwhile in the chocolate market, Cadbury began its LT advertising year with a slew of wraps for Crunchie, which had earlier scored 16/20 in the 'not the worst chocolate bar for your health' survey. One of the strap lines should, of course, have read "I wish it *were* Friday", but advertisers often spurn the subjunctive for fear of frightening potential consumers.

Below: This was a wonderful piece of invention which avoided the obvious Frankenstein approach (and copyright problems) by creating its own monster to promote the jobs website of the same name. After its Burberry gig, LT605 reappeared so adorned and continued to work on route 159.

Top: Pepe Jeans first appeared as a full wrap in 2015, but here's the 2016 design on LT64 in Westminster. In May, the flag poles were back up for the State Opening of Parliament.

Above: I'm a great fan of regular Kettle crisps, but I don't get all the bonkers flavours. I mean, Mozzarella & Pesto Lentil Curls – what they? The green version of Kettle Bites, promoting the lentils, appeared on LT501 amongst others. Vauxhall Cross.

Left: Michael Kors stores also appeared as a full wrap in 2015, so here's the 2016 design on LT308 at Trafalgar Square. The Cockspur Street stops are another spot where lots of subjects stand still long enough for uncluttered photos . . . sometimes.

Above: As a brief diversion from LTs, here's a couple more back wraps at the Muswell Hill stand of route W7: VW1273, Martyn Gerrard estate agency, VW1265, Right Call app.

Right: Save up to £679 on your energy bills - go and live in Spain. There was a rash of these for USwitch in the summer, all of them on non-LTs, such as Westbourne Park's 39114.

Below: More chic for chicks on LT466. You may not have heard of the Coach fashion house but the company has a surprising numbers of branches nationwide, as well as prestige outlets in New Bond Street and Regent Street. Very tasteful.

Above: LT780 entered service in this vinyl wrap which, after a close look, resembles your granny's wallpaper. Tanqueray is a quite expensive dry gin, produced in the home of whisky – Scotland. Pershonally, I don' care where ish moo-ed . . .

Below: OMG, what another mess. This ad promoting holidays in Switzerland could have been really attractive, but what was that pink panel all about? LT59 poses outside a big church in June.

Left: And finally in VV Part One, more booze. Old Mout Cider ads appeared everywhere in the summer to promote a traditional English drink brewed in New Zealand. Go figure. I particularly liked the 'spare wheel' on the back, reminiscent of a Landie and other Chelsea Tractors.

Re-creating Routes

HERE's a quick look at the two TfL-inspired events in 2016 (yes, I know there are lots of route re-creations at Country Area bus rallies and garage open days, but this isn't meant to be a heritage publication).

The first took place on 14th May to mark the 60th anniversary, to the day, of the last London RTW working - RTW467 on route 95 from Brixton garage.

Top of page: The event was masterminded by the RTW Group and, with Arriva's assistance, the runners congregated in early afternoon at the old Tram Depot on Brixton Hill. So, left to right: RTW467, RTW29, RTW185, RTW335 and, sliding into position, RTL1076. If you look closely you can see the old tram tracks and pointwork, although I doubt much of it would work today.

Above: RTW335 motors along Streatham Hill on a short route 95 working to Telford Avenue.

Right: Some chaps with cameras worship at the altar of the Titan. The former-LCC Tramways depot is still used as an overnight out-station, but it's locked most of the time.

RED ARROW
500 Oxford Street Marble Arch
VICTORIA STN

6D PIECE PAY AS YOU ENTER

LONDON TRANSPORT

THE brief road runs of 18th April commemorated the 50th anniversary of the first Red Arrow routes in London - a network that initially blossomed but then withered down to only two. Even so, today's 507 & 521 follow the same concept - short distance, high density - but operate largely for commuters rather than a mix of customers.

To do things properly, the almost-restored AEC Merlin, MBA444, turned out and ran alongside the modern-day Mercedes equivalent, in this case MEC50 in a pseudo-Red Arrow look. Both buses started from Horseferry Road (where there's an original flag and e-plate at the top of one post), and ran first to Waterloo (photo stop) and Victoria (another photo stop). The short day ended with a run from Victoria bus station to Marble Arch, the original routeing of the 500.

Above: The Merlin is overtaken by slightly more up-to-date technology after another photo stop at Queen Elizabeth Gate in Park Lane.

Top of page: MBA444 draws in behind MEC50 beside the Shergar memorial at Marble Arch.

Left: And for nostalgics, the original blue route blind of the early RAs, and the PAYE legend carried by the Merlins. Pay As You Enter was an alien concept in 1966, as much as a sixpence is an alien concept today. If you didn't have a 'tanner', there was only one option . . . and I don't mean contactless payment.

MONTHS five and six produced only nine new contracts and one LT conversion, but they were no less interesting for that. Even the renewals/changes with so-called existing fleet were noteworthy, although route 25 remained in a kind of limbo until firm decisions about the 're-alignment' of its workings.

After the surprise decision to award route 69 and the Virtual Electric E400s to Tower rather than the incumbent Stagecoach, the contract changeover was brought forward to 25th February rather than have joint operation until the official renewal date in June.

To balance things up, the route 26 contract change was also brought forward to February, which meant Tower handing over earlier than expected to CT Plus. However, Hackney's new vehicles had been programmed for build closer to the proper date – hence the hiring of existing Enviro400s to the new operator.

This had happened before, you will recall, when Stagecoach Tridents were temporarily transferred to Tower operation for the 69. Each of the latest loan buses had a professionally-produced ON HIRE label fixed to a nearside window with black sticky tape.

In the event, the second order for the Enviro 400H City began to arrive a little early, so the first, 2501, was in service by the 10th of June. The whole batch of twenty-one were on the road by 8th July and the loan vehicles returned in ones and twos as the new buses came on-stream. Almost under the radar in the interim period, CT Plus also put out an HTL and all five of its SD OmniCitys on the route for the odd day. The Enviro loans came from the number block DN33629-652, but not all of them appeared as CT vehicles.

Main picture: Full circle, finally: A sparkling 2505 rounds the IMAX roundabout soon after starting another journey from Waterloo. The intentional 'London look' applied to Arriva's opening batch of Citys was continued with this order, so the interior trims – seat covers and mouldings - appear identical.

Meanwhile, Tower's DNs had become regular fixtures on the 69, although the former 26/30 pool was now the 25/30/58/69/308/425 pool – in other words, fully common-user.

Contract Change: Tower Transit (LI) to CT Plus (HK) – 25.6.16
Type Change: Trident/Enviro400 to Enviro 400H City
[2501-2521]

26

ON HIRE TO
C T PLUS
ASH GROVE BUS DEPOT
MARE STREET
HACKNEY
E8 4RH

I should add the words 'in theory' to the type change details as the vehicles displaced from route 229 (WVL350-57) re-entered service at New Cross from the 1st of February, mostly on route 321. It's another garage where the double-deckers form a pool for all routes (apart from the majority of hybrids dedicated to the 436), so day-to-day the 129 sees Enviros and a selection of Volvo B9s, including the Bexleyheath migrants.

Above: Older Volvos continue to appear randomly, like WVL240 at the Greenwich Odeon stop. Locals probably know it better as Nando's. In the background is another MEC on loan from Waterloo to New Cross for the 108. The Mercs continued to appear on the route throughout 2016, but after the Great Electric Influx to the Red Arrow routes became much more common in the 'burbs'.

The loss of the 147 put another dent in Stagecoach's dominance of the East End and, naturally, saw off another batch of the once-all-pervading Trident/ALX combination.

Go-Ahead's takeover of the route called for twenty-plus E400s to be collected from various sources and despatched to River Road (until Rainham closed on 2nd July, the 147 was the only route at the new garage). Initially, a scratch batch was formed from spare vehicles at Camberwell, displaced from the 453 and the 345. Come the route 57 changeover in July, the entire batch of former-345 vehicles was reunited at Merton and the 147 settled down to the much neater grouping of E163-185 inclusive. E202 transferred from Bexleyheath to cover for a broken E181 and was still there at the end of the year. The pool, then, appears to be twenty-four to service a PVR of 21.

Below: A refurbished E185 arriving at Canning Town. It's a far cry from the Marylebone Road and the sylvan splendour of Regent's Park.

Contract Change: Stagecoach EL (WH) to Blue Triangle (RR) – 7.5.16
Type Change: Trident/ALX400 to E40D/Enviro400
[E163-185]

147

IN this round of Ealing area route changes, Metroline suffered a trio of losses to Abellio. All three were originally acquired when First Group sold its entire Centrewest operation, including Greenford garage. However, two of the routes acquired new buses from Abellio at this change; numbers and dimensions as shown.

Above: One of the new intake, 8146, swings right into Teignmouth Gardens soon after starting an E5 journey from Perivale Tesco.

Right & Below: 8870 completes a southbound run at the Haven Green roundabout and, from the old days of Centrewest, DML44111 nears the Greenford crossroads on a moody day in 2011. Twenty of these were based at the local garage for the Es (44109-28) and they became DE1675-94 in Metroline's renumbering. Around seven were off-loaded after the loss of E7, the rest moved to the E6, 95 & 195. Abellio's replacement MMCs have hardly ever strayed from the E7 since new, with only odd appearances on 350 & U9.

Left: Two routes in the Great E Shake-up went double-deck on 28th May. As well as gaining more seats, the E8 was extended from Brentford to Hounslow Bell Corner. Most of the VWs were drafted in from Holloway where, you'll recall, early Trident/Enviros had become spare after the LT conversion of route 91. However, earlier VWs in the 10XX series, delivered to Brentford for the 237, also appear. This, for instance, is VW1060 at the first stop outside Ealing Broadway station.

To clarify the batch details, VW1214/1249/1250/1/2/3/4/5/6/8/9/60/2/3 moved from Holloway to Brentford in May. Of the two missing numbers, 1257 was still at HT in December, 1261 moved to Alperton in September.

Below: Route E9 is now worked by Enviro400 diesels, some transferred from Walworth when the 35 and 40 were lost. 9463, on the stand at Haven Green, last worked a Walworth route on 9th May before heading off to a refurb.

Contract Renewal: Metroline (AH) – 28.5.16
Volvo B9/Eclipse Gemini
(Existing VWs at Brentford and others) **E2**

Contract Change: Metroline West (G) to Abellio (WS) – 28.5.16
Type Change: E200 Dart to E20D 8.9m/Enviro200 MMC
[8142-8154] **E5**

Contract Renewal: Metroline (AH) – 28.5.16
Type Change: MAN 12.240 & Dart/Evolution to Volvo B9/
Eclipse Gemini [VW1249-1263, give or take the odd one] **E8**

Contract Change: Metroline West (G) to Abellio (WS) – 28.5.16
Type Change: E200 Dart to E20D 10.8m/Enviro200 MMC
[8865-8875] **E7**

Contract Change: Metroline West (G) to Abellio (WS) – 28.5.16
Type Change: E200 Dart to Trident/Enviro400
(ex-Walworth routes) **E9**

THE third LT conversion at Battersea in barely six months brought the garage's stock to eighty-five vehicles, providing even more scope for mixing and matching. Many of this latest batch, for instance, started out on route 159 (like the 3's vehicles before them). In the reverse direction, the 159 had surrendered its spare buses to the 211 on Sundays for several weeks before the official date of conversion.

The main picture, however, shows the right bus on the right route – LT779 in Parliament Square. Take a good look at the St Stephen's Tower and its famous clock faces; they're due to disappear under white plastic and scaffolding for three years while the mechanism is fully dismantled and overhauled. Let's hope it's not the same firm that's doing Victoria's booking hall.

Opposite page: Meanwhile back at the buses . . . before the change, the 211 was another of Battersea's Enviro routes, operated with a batch of fifteen Euro-5 vehicles delivered in June 2012. One of them, 9538, motors past a West London football club soon after entering service. It's very quiet around here in the cricket season.

Contract Renewal: Abellio (TF) – 7.5.16
Partial Type Change: Various Dart to
E20D 8.9m/Enviro200 MMC [8138-8141

481

I'm only including the 481 for the sake of completeness because a, it
was yet another MMC conversion and b, a straightforward contract
renewal with new vehicles replacing old – four MMCs to service a PVR
of 4 (very economical). *Below:* Needless to say, there was some swopping
about, so here's one of the new intake in Kingston on the K1 rather than
its intended target. As mentioned earlier, I'm listing these as 8.9 metres
because that's how they're described by ADL although, at an overall
length of 8995mm, they are perilously close to the nine metre description
used by others. Does five millimetres matter? Some obviously think so.

Contract Renewal: Tower Transit (LI) – 25.6.16
Volvo B9TL/Eclipse Gemini 2 [VN36101-165]

25

I'm only including the 25 because its renewal date fell in the May/June
period, although the future pattern of service still needs to be pinned
down (there are various stories about splitting the route into sections to
make it less unwieldy and improve time-keeping).

The PVR was raised to 64 from early June, making the 25 the
undisputed size champion in TfL Land. The former leader, route 38, now
operates with a miserable total of 52 buses.

In 2016, a refurbishment programme began for the sixty-five vehicles
ordered by First Group at the 25's last contract change in 2011. In the
process, they've acquired Tower seat covers but retained the blue poles.

The Volvo B5L Hybrid: *Much in Demand*

IN an early edition of Red All Over, and therefore the early days of double-deck hybrids, a summary appeared to illustrate the 'race' between ADL's Enviro400H and the Wright-bodied Volvo hybrid. Assuming it *was* a race, which I doubt, ADL drew into an early lead and maintained it until around 2014.

Since then, the combined orders of Go-Ahead, Metroline, London United and others have reversed the position and the Volvo-powered bus is now numerically superior. Numbers have been further boosted in the past twelve months by the first non-Wright bodies on the Volvo chassis: ADL has supplied batches of Enviro MMCs married to the B5LH rather than its own hybrid platform and, as you will have gathered from reading this edition, the first wave of a substantial invasion of MCV-bodied vehicles has arrived.

All of this begs the question of why the Volvo hybrid chassis has become so popular with London operators. Is it price, reliability, running costs, ease of maintenance, product support or some other factor? From the operators I've contacted, it becomes clear that each company has its own set of criteria. So, it could be all of the above, or something specific. For instance, when I asked one senior manager "Why the Volvo?", he replied candidly: "Because it works."

That may be all we need to know, so let's summarise the main players before considering the SRM variant and the ADL-bodied vehicles.

Arriva

The first London operator of the B5LH evaluated all the double-deck hybrid options in 2009 before settling upon the Volvo as its preferred choice. The initial order for six trials buses (HV1-6) was followed within a year by a first order for production vehicles (HV7-26), all of which began their working lives on route 76. Arriva says the decision was based on "the investment and development that had gone into the product" as well as "the support and maintenance the manufacturer offered" for the new technology.

These early batches were so successful in service that repeat orders took the total fleet to 152 Euro-5 vehicles by 2014. Without the mass influx of New Routemaster hybrids onto Arriva routes, it is likely that many more of the Volvo/Gemini combination would have been ordered. Even so, the substantial batches for London, as well as Arriva's regional businesses, have resulted in a close working relationship with Volvo which has inevitably led to further orders. As things stand, another 123 are in the pipeline for new contracts on routes, 2, 19, 242, 249 & 259 from early 2017.

Above: HV1, the first of many, on its regular beat in Aldwych.

Go-Ahead

The London Central operation took an initial batch of sixteen Gemini 2 hybrids for route 12 on the cusp of construction regulations changing from UK to EC spec. This first batch was built earlier than required (to UK spec) and has remained an anomaly. From WHV17 onwards, all have been built to the revised European Whole Vehicle Type Approval.

Go-Ahead considers all the factors listed in the introduction when making its buying decisions, because they each impact on the whole life cost of a vehicle. However, at the same time it is keen to spread orders across the main manufacturers so that "nose to nose" evaluations of different types can take place. In the current year, for example, we have an order split between the ADL400H MMC and the Volvo/EvoSeti for the new contracts on routes 35 & 40 at Camberwell (regarded as "slow speed" routes). More recently the orders for Putney's new contracts have been similarly split, allowing a different evaluation on "higher speed" routes. Early results show there's little difference in fuel economy between the Camberwell variants, which removes another possible restriction on operating a convenient common-user policy.

This comparative approach has resulted in orders for seventy ADL MMC hybrids in the current year alongside those for the Volvo B5.

Metroline

After taking substantial batches of earlier Geminis, the company has been engaged in a major re-equipment programme in north-west London in 2016, involving seventy-seven vehicles for the takeover of route 114 based at Uxbridge and the contract renewal of routes 140/182 at Harrow Weald (pp. 86/87).

Of the earlier batches, the most surprising development was the allocation of hybrids in 2014/15 to the newly-acquired 34 and 125, both operated from Potters Bar. It had been thought that at least some of those batches would be used to upgrade route 82 because it runs into the centre of town, but all have remained steadfastly in the outer suburbs with only rare journeys along the road to Victoria.

Metroline appears to have fallen out of love with the ADL hybrid after ordering substantial numbers for Cricklewood's inner London routes. So far, it has placed only one order for the upgraded MMC to support the contract renewal of route 332.

RATP-Dev

Although two companies are now reunited under one flag, orders for Volvo/Gemini hybrids were placed separately by London United and London Sovereign - hence a solitary batch at Edgware for route 13 (London Sov) and rather more in the west and south-west at Shepherd's Bush, Fulwell, Hounslow Heath and Tolworth (London United).

2016's new development has been the marrying of a short, and partial, New Routemaster body to the Volvo chassis to produce the SRM (see next page). So far, there are only six ordered for Edgware, initially on route 13 although reported to be migrating to the 183.

Above: Crew training on Tolworth's new buses for the takeover of route 85 took place on the 131, so here's VH45180, 167 & 174 between trips at Fairfield bus station ten days before switching to the 85.

Tower Transit

The order for hybrids for the takeover of the 212 at the start of 2015 provided another surprise because this route, too, is confined to the outer limits of the TfL area. The eleven 'interim' Gemini 3s have rarely strayed from their proper route. At the opposite end of TfL Land, route 328 has been upgraded with new model Gemini 3s in 2016 (see p.38)

Volvo-powered hybrids will finally come to route 82, mentioned earlier, when Tower takes over the contract in April 2017, although the new vehicles are likely to be EvoSetis rather than Geminis.

Below: This portrait of Tower's VH38104 illustrates the combination of features applied to the interim Gemini 3 until StreetDeck look-alikes came along at the end of 2015. You'll have noticed on the opposite page that the trials vehicles also had to make do with 'one front back'.

On the 16th of March, Wrightbus, Volvo, London United and TfL jointly launched the SRM variant at Covent Garden, a shortened version (10.6 metres) of the regular New Routemaster, but built on the Volvo B5LH chassis. At the time, the reasoning was two-fold: ADL had earlier launched the Enviro400H City, a project encouraged by TfL aimed at creating a distinctive 'London look' vehicle. The SRM was presented as Wrightbus's version of the London look, but with one eye on the restricted routes problem that ST812 was meant to tackle. Six SRMs were ordered initially by London United, with a planned introduction date of September on route 13.

Since the launch, it's all gone a bit low-key; the in-service date of VHR45203 (the vehicle shown here) slipped until late-November and only three others had made it onto the road by the end of the year. The anticipated extra orders from London United and other operators haven't materialised yet and, lurking in the background, is the mayor's obvious distaste for the New Routemaster project generally. The fact that the SRM *isn't* an NRM may make no difference.

I also wonder if Wrightbus needs this combination anymore, when the Gemini 3 on the Volvo chassis has been such a runaway success with London operators. True, the SRM offers them a wider choice, but the company may look for substantial orders rather than allow small batches to disrupt the mass production of its headline vehicles.

In the meantime (*top picture*), here's 45203 in its first week of service at the Cockspur Street stop by Trafalgar Square. The 13 shares this stop with full-size LTs on routes 3, 12, 88, 159 & 453 and you would be amazed how many people walk to the back of the SRM, expecting to find a third door! On the right is the restyled rear panel of the launch bus outside the London Transport Museum.

To ride on, the new combination is just as smooth and comfortable as any other Volvo hybrid and the interior is, of course, beautifully finished.

Volvo B5LH - Summary by Operator and Body Type

		Body	Config.	New	Fleet nos.	Batch	Garage	Ordered for route(s)	Notes
Arriva London									
North	10.4m	Gemini 2	39/21	April-June 09	HV1-6	6	AR	76	1
North	10.4m	Gemini 2	39/21	Dec 10/Jan 11	HV7-26	20	AR	76	1
North	10.4m	Gemini 2	39/21	June/July 11	HV27-46	20	SF	73	1
North	10.5m	Gemini 2	39/21	Nov 12-Jan 13	HV47-81	35	SF	73	
North	10.5m	Gemini 2	39/21	May 13	HV82-83	2	SF	73	
North	10.5m	Gemini 2	39/21	May-Nov 13	HV84-131	48	WN	29	2
South	10.5m	Gemini 2	39/21	Jan-March 14	HV132-152	21	BN	59/319	
						152			
Go-Ahead									
Ldn Central	10.4m	Gemini 2	39/21	Sep/Oct 11	WHV1-16	16	Q	12	1
Ldn General	10.5m	Gemini 2	39/21	Feb/March 12	WHV17-31	15	SW	19	
Ldn General	10.5m	Gemini 2	39/21	Oct 12	WHV32-41	10	AF	22	
Docklands	10.5m	E400H MMC	41/22	June 15	EHV1-16	16	SI	135	
Ldn General	10.6m	Gemini 3	41/21	Aug/Sep 15	WHV42-80	39	C	119/202	
Ldn General	10.6m	Gemini 3	41/21	Nov 15-Jan 16	WHV81-104	24	AL	155	
Ldn General	10.6m	Gemini 3	41/21	Dec 15-Jan 16	WHV105-110	6	A	93	
Ldn Central	10.5m	EvoSeti	41/21	April 16	MHV1-20	20	Q	40	
Ldn Central	10.5m	EvoSeti	41/21	Sept-Dec 16	MHV56-85	30	Q	185	
Ldn General	10.6m	int Gemini 3	39/21	Oct 16	WHV111	1	MW	1	
Ldn General	10.6m	Gemini 3	41/21	Oct/Nov 16	WHV143-157	15	MW	1	
Ldn Central	10.5m	EvoSeti	41/21	Oct-Dec 16	MHV21-55	35	PM	63	
Ldn General	10.6m	Gemini 3	41/21	Oct 16-	WHV112-142	31	AF	74/430	
Ldn General	10.6m	Gemini 3	41/21	Oct 16-	WHV158-167	10	AF	74/430	
						268			
Metroline									
Travel	10.5m	Gemini 2	39/21	Oct 12	VWH1360-1364	5	HT	24	
Travel	10.5m	Gemini 2	39/21	Jan-March 13	VWH1408-1419	12	AC	52	
Travel	10.5m	int Gemini 3	41/21	June/July 14	VWH2001-2023	23	PA	7	
Travel	10.5m	int Gemini 3	41/21	Oct-Dec 14	VWH2024-2047	24	PB	34	
Travel	10.5m	int Gemini 3	41/21	Dec 14-Feb 15	VWH2048-2061	14	PB	125	
Travel	10.5m	int Gemini 3	41/21	May/June 15	VWH2088-2121	34	AC	6	
West	10.6m	Gemini 3	41/21	Oct/Nov 15	VWH2122-2144	23	WJ	295	
West	10.6m	Gemini 3	41/21	Aug 16	VWH2167-2186	20	UX	114	
Travel	10.6m	Gemini 3	41/21	Aug-Nov 16	VWH2187-2243	57	HD	140/182	
						212			
RATP-Dev									
Ldn Sovereign	10.5m	Gemini 2	39/21	July/Aug 13	VH1-23	23	BT	13	
Ldn United	10.5m	int Gemini 3	39/21	April/May 15	VH24-43	20	HH	285	
Ldn United	10.5m	int Gemini 3	39/21	July/Aug 15	VH44-52	9	HH	116/285	
Ldn United	10.6m	Gemini 3	41/21	Feb-April 16	VH45153-66	14	S	94	
Ldn United	10.6m	Gemini 3	41/21	April/May 16	VH45167-82	16	TV	85	
Ldn United	10.6m	Gemini 3	41/21	June-Sep 16	VH45183-202	20	S	72	3
Ldn Sovereign	10.6m	SRM	45/21	June & Oct 16	VHR45203-208	6	BT	13	
UMC	11.4m	Gemini 3	45/28	Oct 16	VH45209-213	5	NC	ku	4
						113			
Stagecoach									
Selkent	10.5m	int Gemini 3	41/21	Apr-June 14	13001-13032	32	PD	53	
Selkent	10.5m	E400H MMC	41/22	May/June 15	13061-13081	21	PD	177	
Selkent	10.5m	E400H MMC	41/22	Dec 15/Jan 16	13082-13102	21	TL	47	
						74			
Tower Transit									
	10.5m	int Gemini 3	41/21	Feb/March 15	VH38101-111	11	LI	212	
	10.6m	Gemini 3	41/21	March/April 16	VH38112-136	25	AS	328	
						36			

Gemini 2	233		
interim Gemini 3	168	5	
Gemini 3	305	6	
SRM	6		
Enviro400 MMC	58		
EvoSeti	85		
GRAND TOTAL	**855**		

1   10.4 metre Gemini 2s were built to UK ColC spec,
      10.5 metre vehicles and above (all bodies) were built to EC Whole Vehicle Type Approval spec
2   Two HV106s were produced. The first was destroyed by fire while on test in N. Ireland
3   Ordered against contract renewal of route 72 but diverted elsewhere (refer to main text)
4   Operated on Kingston University routes by United Motorcoaches, alongside similar vehicles in RATP's fleet
      in the same number series. They are double-doored so could be converted for TfL use at a later date
5   Interim Gemini 3 has cut-down top-deck windows, Gemini 2-style front panel and a modifed back panel
6   Current model Gemini 3 has a similar body to the StreetDeck but without the glass panel along the stairline

As a comparison, there were 597 double-decks on the ADL hybrid chassis working TfL routes at 31st December.
By adding roughly 850 NRMs at the same date, the total number of diesel-electric d-ds reaches 2,300.

Stagecoach has always been rather cool towards Volvo-powered buses and has only ordered one batch of Geminis with the B5L hybrid chassis. Clearly it is more comfortable with an ADL involvement, which has so far manifested itself in two separate batches of MMCs with the Swedish undercarriage.

The first three pictures were taken at the Falkirk factory in November 2015, just as production of Stagecoach's latest batch was beginning. There were three units in the chassis shop so, in theory, the basis of vehicles 13082/3/4.

Top of page: The chassis as delivered from Gothenburg. Like the ADL version shown in an earlier edition, this is two separate units separated by a spacer plate. Note the additional bars to provide rigidity in transit. Although this is not a view you see every day, it's fairly obvious where all the internal components will fit.

Above: Stairs in Stagecoach colours awaiting fitment. The staircase is a two-piece resin moulding produced in Turkey. The two halves are bonded together, then the treads are fitted. Although the plates are manufactured in Scotland, it's cheaper to send them abroad for the final assembly. The staircase therefore arrives at Falkirk as a finished unit ready for bolting as a single piece to the chassis. All that's needed is a lightweight hoist to lower it into place.

Above right: The mystery of the Volvo B5 hybrid is finally revealed: What looks like a corner cupboard on the lower deck conceals a vertical radiator assembly.

Right: Because of this component layout, both ADL and Wright (and latterly MCV) have had to employ a degree of ingenuity when modifying existing bus bodies to fit. The result is the rather cramped arrangement of the three seats at the back, found on all three variants. This is the interior of 13065, one of the first batch of Volvo/MMCs delivered to Plumstead garage in 2015.

A Brief History of Stagecoach Enviro400s

(since they were last summarised in Red All Over)

I used to feature these regularly but **2015** was such a quiet year for Stagecoach double-deck orders in London - only twenty-nine Enviro400s across three variants - that I didn't bother. However, they did include the last of the so-called classic design, 12364, a single bus ordered as a top-up for Catford, adding to the large number of Euro 6 spec hybrids delivered twelve months earlier.

Later in the year, the MMC variants began with seven diesels (10301-7) on the E40D chassis for North Street's route 498. The other twenty-one (13061-81 for Plumstead route 177) were the Volvo B5L hybrids with MMC bodies mentioned earlier and they followed the same number series as the one-off Gemini 3 batch delivered new to the same garage for route 53. After that, no further Wright-bodied vehicles were ordered by Stagecoach (anywhere, not just in the capital).

By the end of 2015, as you will have read, construction of the second ADL batch had begun. 13082-102 arrived either side of the New Year break and all were in service by the middle of February.

2016: In the spring another big batch of diesels was delivered for the contract renewals of routes 62 & 145 at Barking and 294 at North Street. The 12000 number series resumed with the thirty-six ADL chassis hybrids ordered for yet another upgrade of route 53. Five assorted stragglers followed to meet pvr increases in the Selkent area.

The three separate series you see in London – 10000, 12000, 13000 – slot into the Stagecoach national numbering scheme which identifies vehicles by chassis type. If we had Scania-based Enviros in the capital, like the rest of Britain, they would be 15-something. As it is, we only have the excruciating OmniCitys.

As another reference point, the MMC-bodied 13000s equate to Go-Ahead's EHV type, the latest 12000s are similar to G-A's most recent EHs. No other London operator took delivery of the MMC diesel bus (Stagecoach 10000s) in the current year.

The summary table shows dates, batch numbers, chassis type, garages and routes, and obviously covers both sides of the river:

Stagecoach East London & Selkent – Enviro400 MMCs into service 2016

January / February	13082-102	21	Volvo B5LH	TL	47
April / May	10308-332	25	ADL E40D	BK	62 / 145
April-June	10333-347	15	ADL E40D	NS	294
July / August	12365-400	36	ADL E40H	PD	53
September	10348-350	3	ADL E40D	TL	199
September	12401	1	ADL E40H	TL	47
November	12402	1	ADL E40H	PD	177
	TOTAL	102			

Above: 12402 was one of a pair of top-up orders for south-east London garage. Although linked to a PVR increase on the 177, flexible allocation at Plumstead means it is just as likely to work alongside the similar hybrid batch dedicated to route 53, 12365-400.

SEVENTEEN new contracts began in this period, ten of them involving new vehicles. The majority were ADL models from the home-grown catalogue, but major progress in reducing central London air pollution showed itself at the very end of August. The first two routes in the period, however, were a straight swop between operators in the south-west area.

Contract Change: London United (TV) to London General (AL) – 2.7.16
Type Change: Various to Trident/Enviro400   [E100-128]

57

The 57 began life as an amalgamation of former tram routes in the 1950s. For most of the de-regulated period it had been operated by London United, so this was a major change by any yardstick. It will come as no surprise that a wide range of types appeared during the last two contract periods. *Above:* VE9, loading up in Eden Street Kingston, was one of ten Volvo B7s with East Lancs Vyking bodies displaced from Shepherd's Bush by the loss of route 49. Initially reallocated to Tolworth and Edgware, they later congregated at the northern outpost for the 114, but are now no more.

London General's 2009 Enviro batch – E100-128 – operated route 345 for seven years from two garages – first Stockwell, then Camberwell – but became redundant in April's 35/40/345 swop-around. Some transferred to East London to support the newly-acquired 147, others went to

Merton and New Cross, some back to Stockwell. Half-a-dozen that worked the 345 on its last day as a G-A route went off for refurbishment and reappeared 'red all over' on the Wimbledon tennis shuttles at the end of June. *Below Left:* A gleaming E108 sets down another load of rich people at the Somerset Road entrance to the All-England Club.

Come the 57's contract change – and a need to service a PVR of twenty-seven – the strays magically re-formed in their original group at Merton where all appeared on the new route within a few days. Because of their temporary missions elsewhere, most were not refurbished, and so began their new assignment in the full livery of Go-Ahead they had worn since new. *Below:* E105 pulls away from the Wimbledon station stop. Within a short time, Merton's common-user policy showed itself and Enviros of similar spec from the 118 batch – E138-150 – also appeared on the 57.

Contract Change: London General (AF) to London United (TV) – 2.7.16
Type Change: Volvo B7/Eclipse Gemini & others to Volvo B5LH/Gemini 3
[VH45167-182]

85

Comments about London United's longevity as operator of the 57 apply even moreso to Putney garage, which had maintained an allocation for route 85 on and off since 1935. True, London United ran the route in the early years of the new century, but Putney and Go-Ahead had been in full control since 2004. (I could rattle on here for some distance about the allocations once based at the long-defunct Putney Bridge and Norbiton garages for the 85, but I'm constantly reminded about 'overdoing' south London in this series in the interests of 'balance' . . . which is why I have to go to places like Essex.)

Above: The old 85, as we must now call it, is represented by one of numerous Volvo B7/Geminis on Putney's books. WVL69 turns into the start of Eden Street, the bit nobody photographs, soon after setting off for

Putney Bridge. [BTW, if you look closely at the optician's chart on the far right, you will see it reads John Rose Eyecare. If you *can't* read it . . .]

As Tolworth garage had to wait until the contract date to get its paws on the 85, vehicle testing and driver training on the new type took place on the 131, as shown earlier (this may also have called for some route learning). All but one of the sixteen new vehicles first appeared in this way.

Below: At the northern end of route 85, VH45181 poses outside the photogenic Green Man pub on Putney Heath. Shame about all the street furniture. Around eleven of the new batch appeared on the route on the first day. Until the whole lot had been retrieved from the 131, Tolworth deployed Scania OmniCitys to make up the numbers (from the early batch with the concrete seats. Lovely.)

Contract Renewal: London United (TV) – 2.7.16
Type Change: Various Dart/Pointer to E20D 10.8m/Enviro200 MMC
[DE20129-42]

265

Above: In the same area, Tolworth garage acquired even more new vehicles with the 265's contract renewal. As you must know what a single-deck MMC looks like by now, here's one of the eclectic mix found on the route before the change: DPS653 dives under the A3 trunk road to reach the stops outside the Roehampton Asda. The northbound 85 also performs this manoeuvre. In the background, one of Abellio's E200s waits time before a return journey on Tuesday/Friday mobility route 969.

Below: Putney's VE type, restricted solely to route 85 since new, moved on to Sutton garage and became daily performers on the 213. If you've never travelled on them, VE1-3 are big, growly Volvo B9s wedged inside

Enviro400 bodies. In London and everywhere else they remain unique, and should be admired for their 'different-ness'.

Sadly, they are now beginning to look like every other Enviro as refurbishments sweep away their stripes. I was surprised, then, to find VE1 still in original paint in December. This is the southern terminus of the 213 in Bushey Road, Sutton, outside the home garage.

Incidentally, although the DOE type predominates at Sutton, a common user policy with the small batches of Enviro400s and Presidents means they can also appear daily on any of the garage's routes . . . and do. Refurbishment of the seven-year-old Optare-bodied Tridents began soon after the 213's contract renewal (see *Quite Interesting*).

Contract Renewal: London General (A) – 2.7.16
Renewed with 'existing fleet' vehicles,
but with a partial type change

213

Contract Renewal: Stagecoach Selkent (PD) – 23.7.16
Type Change: Volvo B5LH/Gemini 3 to Volvo B5LH/Enviro400 MMC
[12365-400]

53

Following on from the Stagecoach Enviro summary, here's route 53's latest upgrade to coincide with route 53's latest contract. Like before, more new kit at Plumstead provoked another bout of cascading from one side of the river to the other. On this occasion, the solitary batch of Gemini-bodied Volvo hybrids (13001-32) cascaded onto other Plumstead routes, freeing up 'classic model' Enviro400s to cross to West Ham to upgrade route 86 . . . consigning yet another batch of ALX400/Tridents to the dustbin.

Above: Here's one of the new intake, 12368, turning into St George's Road from the re-modelled Elephant & Castle roundabout. The blind shows a qualifier in capitals spreading to non-LTs – an increasing trend as the year wore on.

Below: As Stagecoach's once-massive early Trident fleet is now under serious threat, let us not waste an opportunity to show one of the 10.5 metre examples from the Transbus era: 17765 turns at the Mercury Gardens roundabout in Romford shortly before completing its journey at the station. By the end of August, the daily composition of route 86 was roughly two-thirds Enviro, one-third ALX400 . . . all Tridents, of course, as the transferred E400s were UK spec vehicles rather than EC spec on the E40D chassis.

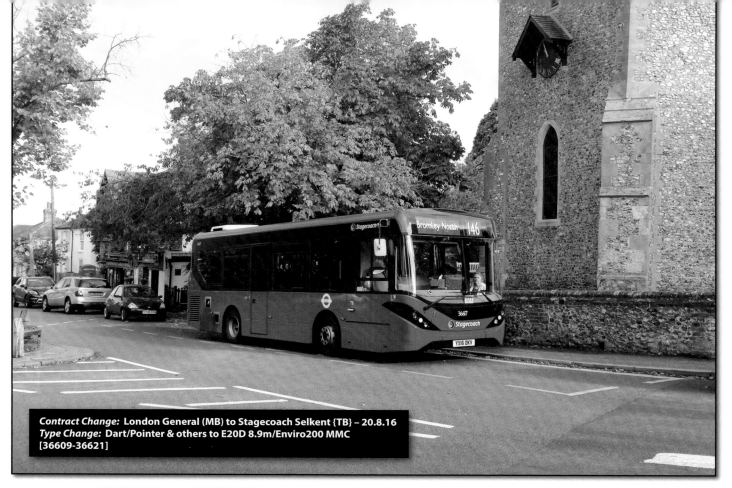

Contract Change: London General (MB) to Stagecoach Selkent {TB} – 20.8.16
Type Change: Dart/Pointer & others to E20D 8.9m/Enviro200 MMC
[36609-36621]

146   336

This is the change of two linked routes from former-Metrobus to Selkent, achieved with a batch of thirteen MMCs ordered for Bromley garage. Previously, Pointers from the batch 271-286 were daily performers on the 336, but almost anything single-deck from Orpington's allocation was likely to appear (apart from the Solos, obviously). The PVR of the two routes is 10 +1, so thirteen buses may look a little generous.

The one-bus route, the 146, runs from Bromley North station to the village of Downe near Biggin Hill. The service is hourly, with only a five-minute turnaround at each end, so a solitary single-decker is more than adequate. Having said that, it wasn't unusual for the Metrobus garage mto swop vehicles around during the day, a practice continued on occasions since Stagecoach's takeover.
Above: From the new group, 36616 takes its turn on the Downe run. After arriving from Bromley, the dedicated bus waits time at the stop beside St Mary's Church. The clock tells you this will be the 11.00 departure.

Slightly more straightforward was the replacement of route 377's old Darts based at Enfield with MMCs. *Right:* From the middle period of the previous contract, this is PDL142 on the Oakwood station stand at the western end of the route. Although displaced by the new intake at the end of June, this bus miraculously re-surfaced at Dartford two months later, working peak hour journeys on route B13.

Contract Renewal: Arriva LN (E) – 9.7.16
Type Change: Dart/Pointer to E20D 8.9m/Enviro200 MMC
[EN34-38]

377

Above: Before the change of motive power, 9471 completes another journey at Clapham Junction, ignoring the bus lane because it's about to turn right onto the stand. Many moons ago the two-bus parking area the 344 uses at the top of St John's Hill was the entrance forecourt to the LSWR's Clapham station, with a pedestrian walkway above what is now platform 9 & 10. You can still see the remains of the original supporting girders protruding from under the bridge. The refurbished building in the background is the one-time LB&SCR station entrance.

Although the 344 contract was a renewal rather than an operator change, the new vehicles appeared in timely fashion and almost all were in service in the week leading up to 20th August. There were a few stray workings on other routes, like the 452 & C2, but a concentration of the batch onto the 344 quickly became the norm. Curiously, there were only eighteen MMCs against a PVR of 25, but this can be partly explained by the transfer of older hybrids from Walworth to Battersea after the 30th April changes.

The 344 is normally the only route to cross Southwark Bridge, but the path of northbound journeys out of Upper Thames Street was blocked by major building work in 2016. The river crossing therefore became London Bridge, after a detour along Southwark Street, with line of route regained at Monument station.

Left: Southbound buses continued as before, diving down to the embankment past the stone column commemorating the Great Fire of London, and continuing via Southwark Bridge. This is 2543 in Fish Street Hill.

Fall-Out: Twenty Euro-4 diesel Enviros, 9467-9486, were withdrawn from Battersea at the end of August as a direct result of the 344 upgrade. They were originally delivered in August 2009 as part of a larger batch of 38 (9467-9504) for routes 156 and 344. By December, a small number of the early ones began to pitch up at Sullivan's, replacing older kit like ALX400s.

This change was a little baffling, as the contract date came and went and the intended refurbished Gemini 2s remained on route 2 (see *Quite Interesting*). However, from 9th September they moved en masse to the 417, with only the occasional VLA and T thereafter, while the 2 reverted to its former diet of VLA, with only the occasional refurb.

Above: So, ignoring all that and treating this like a perfectly ordinary changeover, here's the Before - VLA43 running along a short stretch of Rookery Road, Clapham Common, to reach the stand at Old Town. A summer shower momentarily darkens the sky.

Below: And the After - DW285 glows in autumn sunshine after assuming its rightful route. There were fourteen in all, DW249 & 277-289, and all reappeared in the modified red front-look first seen on WDL1 and the route 13 Geminis. Inside they looked like new – pristine blue moquette – and still felt like new – absolutely no padding on the seats.

Contract Change: London General (C) to Arriva LS (TH) – 27.8.16
Type Change: Various to Trident/Enviro400
'existing fleet'

64

Before Croydon garage migrated from the banner of Metrobus to that of London General, the 64 was a daily mixture of Scania types. With the change of operator (and clearly a change of emphasis), more conventional G-A power began to appear, including a batch of Presidents displaced from Merton alongside the occasional Volvo hybrid borrowed from route 119. *Above:* PVL377, crossing the railway at East Croydon, is typical of the final months of operation before the route was lost.

Arriva re-jigged much of its Enviro400 collection to facilitate the changeover and vehicles appeared from near and far on the first day - not only from 'down the road' at South Croydon but also from the former allocation of route 341 at Tottenham. By filling the gaps in its existing number range, Thornton Heath ended up with T118-167 inclusive (plus the early batch T12-26 brought in from Barking for the 198) to service its three double-deck routes – that's sixty-five vehicles for a combined PVR of 56. Expect any to appear on any, thanks to common-user.

Below: To illustrate the first point, here's T120, originally a South Croydon bus, and T150 from the 341 batch. Both are in the process of running round the block after their last stop at Thornton Heath Pond, so-called. In case you're wondering, the bus on the left is stationary after the traffic came to a sudden stop.

Other Contract Renewals with 'existing fleet'
in the July/August period

Route 65	London United (FW)	2.7.16
Scania OmniCity & others		[PVR 27]
Route 371	London United (FW)	2.7.16
E200 Dart/Enviro200H & others		[PVR 13 + 2]
Route K5	Quality Line (EB)	2.7.16
Optare Solo M880		[PVR 6]

Despite the 'existing fleet' tag, four of the spare Volvo/Gemini hybrids ordered for route 72, VH45183-6, ended up at Fulwell for the 65. Unless a remedy can be found for the parlous state of Hammersmith Bridge (see later), the quartet may remain on the 65 forever . . . or they may not (see later also).

Bottom of page: The five hybrid Dart Enviros continued to appear on the 371 in 2016, although they were 'pinched' for the temporary Petersham diversion routes in August. HDE5 negotiates the section before it was closed. This early hybrid batch is seven years old now and must be due for either refurbishment or reassignment.

And finally (not that there's room for a picture) the K5. The longest of the Kingston Ks, at twelve miles, winds its way from Ham Common to Morden via a selection of 'big railway' stations – Kingston, Norbiton, New Malden (almost), Motspur Park, Raynes Park and Wimbledon Chase. Optare Solos predominate, but other single-deckers from Epsom's collection are commonplace. If you're planning a trip, be warned: the K5 runs half-hourly and its route is highly convoluted . . . which means you probably won't have a clue where you are.

Below: The old 65, and the current 65 for that matter, is represented by SP26 (now renumbered as SP40026). The bus is standing roughly in the space once occupied by Kingston down goods yard, from where the land was dug out to provide a second railway crossing on the west side of the station. I would call it an over-the-top solution, but for the fact that it goes underneath.

ON Tuesday, 30th August, SEe4, 5, 7 & 9 became the first of the production batch of BYD electric vehicles to enter service on the Red Arrow routes - an event much anticipated by some after a lengthy period of trial running by EB1 & 2 (also from BYD) and EI 1 & 2 (supplied by Irizar). First out was SEe9 on the 507 at 0738 and SEe5 on the 521 at 0747. One hour later, SEe7 joined in and obligingly passed my camera in late-afternoon at the IMAX roundabout (*above*).

507	Contract Renewals: London General (RA/MW) – 27.8.16 Type Change: Mercedes Citaro to BYD D9UR 12m/Enviro200 EV [SEe1-51]	521

Although South Croydon's route 312 was the first to become wholly electric, zero-emissions vehicles were also running by this time on the H98 (London United), 69 (Tower Transit), 98 (Metroline) and RV1 (Tower again) - with varying degrees of consistency. The conversion of two major, and intensely busy, central London routes represented another step forward in tackling the capital's air quality challenge.

Of course, a comparative handful of non-diesel buses won't make a scrap of difference when there are zillions of taxis and commercials clogging up our airways, but it is a requirement of all progress that activity must begin somewhere. Remember how quickly the hybrid fleet expanded after a tentative start.

The original plan was for Waterloo garage to change from diesel to electric 'in one hit', using the Bank Holiday weekend of August 27th-29th as a convenient window. That would have involved ripping out all the diesel fuelling equipment and replacing it with charging sockets – enough to cater for fifty-one replacement vehicles – but it proved impossible logistically. One problem was said to be finding enough low-loaders and tow vehicles to shift the new buses to the sockets in time to ensure a full service on both routes on the Tuesday morning. To quote a famous line from a famous film - *"There's still a million things that could go wrong with this stunt"* - so commonsense and practicality dictated a managed cascade.

Another constraint was the limited time available to take up the massive power increase needed for daily charging. If this hadn't happened within a fixed period, the National Grid would have diverted the extra power to the next applicant in line – such is the level of demand in big cities.

Below: Mention has been made of the first use of a lower case 'e' to denote an electric variant within Go-Ahead's usual numbering convention, but it may be something else not to lose sleep over.

ENVIRO 200 EV

The fifty-one vehicles were constructed at ADL's Falkirk plant by marrying a version of the MMC single-deck body to ready-made chasses shipped in from the Far East. The roof pod panel suggests ADL is presenting the combination as its MMC electric vehicle, which might be a little unwise. Like the awful EBs before them, the ride of this batch of Chinese chasses is best described as rigid, sometimes uncomfortably so. Even ADL's careful coachwork was groaning and squeaking within days, so it will be interesting to see what shape the bodywork is in after five years of hacking to and from Waterloo.

Compounding the rigidity problem is a high unladen weight, shown on a side panel as 12115kg. Compare this with the New Routemaster, which weighs in between 12095 and 12400 kg, or the Enviro400 MMC at around 11700 kg (you may also have noticed these are double-deckers) and the extent of the problem becomes clear. Yet despite all this portliness crashing over the potholes, the BYD is allowed to carry 93 passengers (21 seated, 72 standing), plus a driver, giving a maximum gross weight of just over 18.5 tonnes!

Time will tell whether I am being harsh (like the ride) or whether acquiring this technology from overseas was the wrong decision.

In the meantime, a question to the mayor's office, who started this particular ball rolling: Doesn't Mercedes make an electric bus?

Below: On the positive side, there are innovations to be welcomed, not least the excellent information screens first trialled on one of route 360's hybrids. As well as next stop details and a full route map, with times to every stop, Underground service updates appear on one of the alternating screens. Waterloo-bound journeys can also display times of the next SouthWest Trains departures. The 507's buses heading for Victoria have shown the enigmatic clock on Southern's strike days.

Bottom right: Plug in your life support here. There are USB sockets in the backs of the rear seats in which passengers may charge their phone battery although, as others have pointed out, journeys on the 500s tend to be quite short. My best score was +4% between Victoria and Waterloo. You should get more if you turn off the screen while charging.

Bottom Left: Because the bodywork is essentially an Enviro200 MMC, there is the standard 'theatre' style layout at the back, which means we've also lost the sociable seating arrangement of the Citaro.

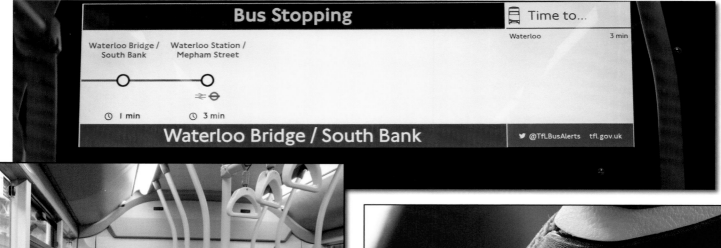

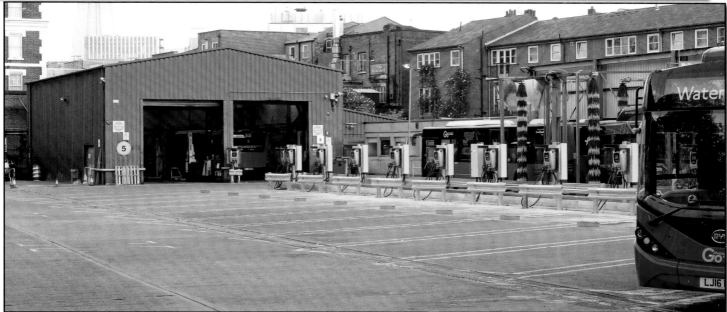

Top of page: The revised Waterloo garage layout in October – lots of charging points and a handful of new deliveries waiting to enter service. On the far right is SEe10, one of five decked out in Green Bus vinyls.

Above: The view from the other side of the site shows the 'herringbone pattern', or echelon parking, of the new arrangement. These shots were taken in late-afternoon, when most of the fleet had vanished to work the evening peak. On Mondays-Fridays, between forty-four and forty-seven vehicles work the two routes in the rush hours; during the day, it's no more than eight on each.

Left: The individual charging stands appear identical to those installed when the BYD trials vehicles arrived three years ago. There are forty-three in total here and five more to be installed at Mandela Way, suggesting that Waterloo will remain closed on Saturdays and Sundays and the other garage will continue to work the weekend 507.

Fall-Out:

By the end of the year, 45 electric vehicles were in service, although SEe1 & 2 remained invisible. The 50-strong MEC fleet continued its haphazard reallocation to other work and other areas as follows:
- 18 had become new entrants on route 108 at New Cross, most but not all refurbished and 'up-seated' from 21 to 29 at H&D Eastleigh
- 7 remained at Waterloo/Mandela Way, primarily for the weekend 507
- 16 were in limbo, some not having worked either Red Arrow route since October, and
- 9 were shown as withdrawn, some from the old 108 allocation.

Of the 'spares', eight were reported to be transferring to City of Oxford services, but the six earmarked for the schooldays 646 & 648, based at River Road, remained in the pool. Apparently, 12 metres of length was more than the routes could cope with.

By the time you read this, the final allocation of the Citaros should have become clearer.

Farnborough 2016

Welcome to
FARNBOROUGH

Proud to be the birthplace of British aviation
Borough of Rushmoor

THE biennial Farnborough Air Show, the 'shop window' for the British aerospace industry, took place from Tuesday, July 12th, to Sunday the 17th. As in previous years, Go-Ahead London's Commercial Services division provided the Park & Ride shuttles from the Queen's Parade site to the airfield bus station with an eclectic mix of dedicated CS fleet vehicles backed up by front-line buses from south London garages. Stagecoach Provincial sent along a mix of Tridents and Enviro400s for the railway station trips.

Opposite page top: E283, one of Comm. Svcs.' 10.9 metre Enviro400s, sets off from the boarding point at Queen's Parade well-loaded on the Friday, when industry professionals mingled with enthusiasts who'd paid a premium entry fee to avoid the public crush of Saturday and Sunday. E282 waits behind. Note the dot matrix destinations screens - *verböten* in TfL Land but pretty much standard in the CS fleet.

Centre: WVL83 completes its journey at the bus station, closely pursued by Putney's WVL504. Among the other runners on this particular day were WVL19, WVL272, WVL508, PVL221, MEC33 and former-Metrobus 946.

Bottom Left: LDP201, on the other hand, was one of several single-deckers allocated to a shuttle service inside the airfield perimeter for companies' staff working at the event.

Below: Not running on this day was Go-Ahead's newly-acquired Volvo/Gemini hybrid demonstrator BX14TJV, carrying the number 111. This somewhat enigmatic appearance provoked some head-scratching at the time until the magic of the web revealed the bus's history (stints in Dublin and the West Midlands). Unusually for a general-purpose demonstrator it was built with two doors so, like the two Volvo diesels created specifically for London trials, it was ripe for takeover by a

London operator. When CS had finished using it as a shuttle bus, WHV111 resurfaced as Mandela Way's trainer before the introduction of Volvo hybrids to route 1. It surfaces again on page 103.

Top of this page: For fans of the provincial, here's two of the Stagecoach buses working shuttles at Farnborough's main line station - 15843 from Dover and 17670 from just about everywhere.

All Change - September/October

THIS two-month period begins with the type change that wasn't – the aborted plan to upgrade route 72 to double-deck because of continuing 'issues' with Hammersmith Bridge. A game of musical buses then ensued . . .

The 72 is worked almost entirely by 02-reg. 10.1 metre Dart SLF/Pointers based at Shepherd's Bush, although early Enviro200s can appear. The PVR is 28 and the service is, shall we say, frequent. Replacing the fourteen-year-old Darts is clearly a priority and the plan to double-deck the route at this contract renewal would have increased capacity while significantly lowering the vehicle requirement. However, there are stringent operating restrictions on Hammersmith Bridge, including a barrier system at both ends supervised by TfL officials, who ensure only a single bus crosses the decking at any one time.

It is no exaggeration to say the bridge is being shaken apart by the traffic; if you walk across, the ground literally moves beneath your feet whenever a bus or a large van rumbles by. There appear to be only two solutions – a massive and time-consuming strengthening of the 130-year-old structure (which would include replacing the carriageway), or closure of the bridge to motor traffic, including buses. In these cash-strapped times, the latter may be the preferred option, but there is nowhere else for the traffic to go. Putney Bridge, on the eastern side, is already severely congested in peak periods, and Barnes to the west is a railway bridge. The next one down is Chiswick Bridge on the A316, but that's also intensely busy because it connects to the M3 motorway.

As a result, there is pressure for decisions to be made on all fronts, from the age of the current bus fleet to the challenge of saving a Grade II listed building from destruction.

Top Picture: After waiting its turn on the approach to the northern end of the bridge, DPS671 is about to restart as the barrier lifts. The three TfL 'monitors', lurking behind the trees on the right, are in radio contact with a similar number on the southern bank.
Below: DPS650 gingerly makes its way across the battered decking. As well as the 20 mph speed limit, there is a weight restriction of 7.5 tonnes – considerably less than a 10.1 metre Dart.
Below Left: The E-plates on the north side stop reveal the extent of the problem – the 72 has to compete for space with five other daily routes.

BUS STOP
Hammersmith Bridge
North Side

towards
Hammersmith Bus Station
and Shepherds Bush

24 hour	24 hour	
33	**72**	**209**
283	**419**	**485** Monday-Saturday
609 School journeys		

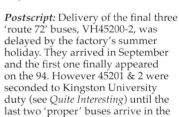

And what of the twenty Volvo hybrids ordered for the route 72 upgrade?

As mentioned earlier, the first four went to Fulwell and appeared on route 65. The rest, VH45187 onwards, crept out in two groups, with the early ones appearing on route 13. Fair enough, we thought, Edgware has a lot of old junk that needs replacing, why not upgrade the 13 and transfer its Gemini 2 hybrids to routes like the 183 & 292? That idea lasted for eight days until buses from the new batch began appearing on route 94 from Shepherd's Bush.

Over four weeks in August, all of 45187-199 either moved south or entered service on the 94 and the similar vehicles formerly working the route, VH45153-166, transferred to Edgware . . . for route 13 . . . but not VH45155.

Above: However, because of this, I can offer you the unrepeatable sight (until another change-round) of one of the latest batch working the 13 during its brief stay at BT. This is Dorset Square on 26th July and VH45194 heading north.

Left: To illustrate the confusion further, these are the operator details on the side of the new batch as delivered to London Sovereign but now working from 'the Bush'. Their replacements from the 94 showed London United's details. And why did this happen? Simply because of 'via blinds' and their position on nearside windows – Shepherd's Bush allocation at the top, Edgware allocation at the bottom, to match the earlier Gemini 2s on route 13 . . . or was it the other way round?

Postscript: Delivery of the final three 'route 72' buses, VH45200-2, was delayed by the factory's summer holiday. They arrived in September and the first one finally appeared on the 94. However 45201 & 2 were seconded to Kingston University duty (see *Quite Interesting*) until the last two 'proper' buses arrive in the spring, apparently.

45183 (originally at Fulwell for the 65) transferred to Tolworth in late-September to join the 85 batch and was still there at the end of the year.

And the rickety bridge? Well, in November Hammersmith & Fulham Council admitted that the £27 million strengthening project would be delayed "until late 2017" because of a budget shortfall, despite the fact that TfL will pick up most of the bill, believed to be around £20 million.

Contract Change: London Sovereign (BT) to Metroline West (UX) – 3.9.16
Type Change: Volvo B7/various to Volvo B5LH/Gemini 3
[VWH2167-2186]

114

If London Sovereign had retained route 114, the 72 saga might have ended differently: its buses might have upgraded another existing route at Edgware. In the event, Metroline West had already won the contract against the promise of new hybrids of similar kind – hence the sweeping away of yet another batch of Volvo B7s.

Above: VLE34 arrives at Queensbury station while heading for Ruislip. The bus made its last trip on the 114 on 13th July and was withdrawn along with thirteen others.

After many weeks of general inactivity on the new bus front, seventeen sparkling hybrids appeared on the first day of the contract, highlighting once again the Metroline paradox. At a contract change, when a squadron introduction is essential, the company rises to the challenge magnificently. Its cascades of new vehicles, on the other hand, last ages.
Below: VWH2175 at the Porlock Avenue stop, a mile or so from Harrow town centre. The only other double-deck route at Uxbridge is the limited stop 607, so there were no stray workings by the new vehicles in the whole of their first month. However, don't rule out one of them making it to White City sometime.

	Contract Renewals: Metroline (HD) – 3.9.16	
140	**Type Change:** Volvo B7/President & others to Volvo B5LH/Gemini 3 [VWH2187-2243]	**182**

This was another glacial changeover from old kit to new, which began in advance of the contract date when about ten vehicles went to work in the space of a fortnight. Then it all stopped, presumably while engineering resources were concentrated on getting the route 114 buses ready. Then, it stayed stopped, as stories of ticket machine shortages emerged once more.

Taking the end of September as a review point, there were twenty working by then as a common-user pool for both the 140 & 182. This had already allowed the standing down of a number of ageing Presidents and the despatch of the 140's small batch of Volvo B9/Geminis to their next assignment. VW1243-48 went to Alperton, where they joined others of similar type on the 83 and new route 483 (see later).

Above: One of the long-serving Presidents, VP626, emerges from Uxbridge Road, Harrow Weald, before turning towards the town.

This is only a short distance from the start of the journey at Oxhey Lane, although the first stop is called Bannister Playing Fields.

Below: The 'isolated' VWH2201 passes Waitrose in South Harrow. The parallel production line effect showed itself again with the delivery of two separate number blocks although, for a time, this one was all on its own in the middle. In the end, the spread of new vehicles entering service stretched from 8th August (VWH2213) to . . . er, well, I had hoped to give you a number and a date here to complete the changeover, but four were still outstanding on 31st December . . . almost four months after the first new bus appeared. I would phone the Guinness Book of Records, but this has happened before with the route 6 changeover in 2015.

Instead, a fact: Fifty-seven Gemini 3s will eventually service a combined PVR of 52 for both the 140 and the 182.

Contract Renewal: Arriva LN (GR) – 3.9.16
Type Change: DB250/ALX400 & Pulsar Gemini to Wright StreetDeck
[SW1-10]

340

Above: A gathering of new paint outside Harrow Weald garage provides a challenge for local motorists. SW9 passes SW10 as VWH2187 pokes through the garage doors before starting another journey on the 140. Note also the off-side of SW10; there is no glass panel following the stair-line. You could argue, then, that these are not 'full-blown' StreetDecks but Gemini 3s with StreetDeck chasses and drive train . . . or you may have better things to do with your time.

Below: As mentioned earlier, Arriva's StreetDeck demonstrator, SW1, went north after it was taken into stock and served as Garston's staff trainer in advance of the nine new vehicles. Although nominally allocated to the route 340 contract, the bus spent a greater part of its early months on the 142 and 258. Here it is at Harrow bus station on 8th September.

New Route: Metroline West (ON) – 3.9.16
**Volvo B9TL/Eclipse Gemini gathered from existing fleet at
Alperton, Holloway & Harrow Weald - PVR 25 (24/18 Sat/Sun)**

483

The new 483 runs from Harrow bus station to Alperton via Wembley Central, then replaces route 83 between Alperton and Ealing Hospital – a total distance of eleven miles at an eight-minute frequency. On a typical day, its buses are a mix of former-First Centrewest Geminis previously allocated to route 83, in the VW17XX number series, and genuine Metroline vehicles (VW12XX) cascaded from genuine Metroline garages. Like the E8 shown earlier, Holloway was a significant donor.

Above: From the former-Centrewest collection, here's VW1760 (formerly VN37781) amid the autumnal shades of Ealing Common. Thirty-one of similar type arrived at Alperton when the route 83 contract was last renewed in 2009. The combined PVR of the re-jigged 83/483 is 44.

As well as a large number of Euro-6 hybrids for the takeover of routes 54 & 75, Catford garage has received smaller batches of diesel Enviros in the recent past to upgrade the 136, and Volvo-powered MMCs for the 47. Although the hybrids mostly stick to their proper routes, any of the garage's Enviro400 collection can appear on any of the double-deck numbers. On a typical day, the 199 enjoys a full spread of ADL variants and will occasionally benefit from the latest trio of Euro-6 diesel MMCs if they're not allocated elsewhere in the run-out. If you like variety, you will fully appreciate a common-user policy; if you don't, you won't.
Below: On the 'correct route', 10350 sets off from Canada Water bus station. The upper case qualifiers march on.

Contract Renewal: Stagecoach Selkent (TL) – 17.9.16
Partial Type Change: Trident/ALX400 to ADL E40D/Enviro400 MMC
[10348-10350]

199

"There is less to this than meets the eye."
THE modified quote of an obscure Hollywood actress perfectly sums up the 1st of October and the period beyond. On paper, the month looked extremely busy, but there was a high degree of 'existing fleet' in the mix, coupled with delays to new vehicles entering service, the everlasting LT conversion of route 189 and the "I suppose it'll happen eventually" of the 253.

Perversely, new vehicles entering service reached three figures, as the huge backlog of previous months began to clear itself.

Do not become too obsessed with dates in this section: Route 1 should have changed over on the 1st but its 10.6 metre Geminis had to soldier on a while longer, not because the replacements vehicles were waiting for Oyster readers and/or ticket machines, but owing to the small matter of not having been delivered. A significant number arrived in October, but there were still gaps in the sequence by mid-November.

Above: Here's one of the oldies: VWL30 pulls into the Waterloo Bridge photographic studio in the autumn of 2014. There were eighteen of this combination on Mandela Way's allocation but wanderings had become almost unheard of, because there was nowhere for them to wander to, not since the 453 converted to LTs. The VWLs were occasionally joined by WVL363, one of the Volvo B9s displaced from Bexleyheath (see earlier). *Below:* Eventually (that word again), the shiny, new Geminis pitched up in ones and twos. Here, for instance is WHV146 setting off from Canada Water bus station on a wild and windy afternoon in November. There are better locations for photos between here and Tottenham Court Road, but the challenge on this particular day was remaining upright.

Contract Renewal: London General (Q) – 1.10.16
Type Change: Various s/d to Volvo B5LH/MCV EvoSeti
[from MHV56-85, but eventually EH113-130]

42

The 42 is slightly trickier to illustrate because you already know what the old route looked like (page 6) and you already know what an Evoseti looks like (front cover onwards). So here's the 42 at its revised northern terminus – a stand in Tower Bridge Road after the route was cut back by the three-month closure of the bridge for maintenance work, the start of which coincided to the minute with the 42's double-decking.

The first day produced a full slew of 'Slabs', some from the newly-delivered batch, some from the 35/40 pool. *Above:* One of the old on the new – MHV13, standing beneath the ten-track approach to London Bridge station. Under the bridge and around the corner, there was a revised final stop for the 42 in Druid Street. The amendment to the southbound journey involved a sideways move to East Dulwich Sainsbury's instead of Denmark Hill.

Below: A spare half-page allows the inclusion of the second route to convert to double-deck on 1st October. The D8's contract had already been extended for two years from 17th September under the Quality Incentive scheme and it continued to operate from the G-A Docklands garage at Silvertown. The previous PVR of 8 appears to have increased, because there were nine double-decks on the route in the following Monday's peak hours.

The buses themselves were 2009-built Scania OmniCitys (from the sequence 958-73), some of which had been displaced from Croydon garage by the loss of route 64 in August. From the transferred batch, and still showing off its Metrobus silver, this is 959 at Westferry Circus.

Contract Renewal: London Central (Q) – 1.10.16
Type Change: Various to Volvo B5LH/MCV EvoSeti
[MHV56-85]

185

The 185 provides another opportunity for a blast from the recent past. Like the old 68, the phrase 'from a host of possibilities' applies here too. Could they both be Camberwell routes, perhaps? I've chosen PVL79, one of the centre stairs Presidents that were regulars on the route until 2013. And as this picture is from 2011, you can see how part of Victoria operated before the chaos of recent years. Around the block, out of sight, work had recently begun on the seven-year booking hall, or the Victoria Underground Station Upgrade as it's officially known.

Before the works, the 185 had its stand here, outside the District Line entrance to the station, and ran round the corner to the first pick-up in Terminus Place – a stop shared by other routes going to Vauxhall like the 2, 36 & 436. Currently the 185 begins its journeys from the Neathouse Place stop, near the 'temporary' stand in Vauxhall Bridge Road.

MHV56-85 were the official allocation against the contract renewal, but the common-user approach at Camberwell will continue to produce a mix of types even when new MMCs arrive for route 42.
Below: This illustrates the point - MHV4, from the 35/40 replacement group, approaches Vauxhall bus station.

And for lovers of the esoteric, consider the twelve-day loan from Mandela Way of WHV144, which worked all manner of Camberwell's double-deck numbers, including the 185, towards the end of November. WHV151 also appeared on the 185, but only for a single day.

Five weeks before the contract date, the 450 transferred to Norwood garage to make room for the newly-acquired route 64 at Thornton Heath. *Above:* From the period before that, here's PDL136 turning at the clock tower. The Pointers remained at TH (mostly working route 410 thereafter) and Norwood put out SB120/Cadets until the new vehicles arrived.

Against expectation, Arriva ordered its first batch of StreetLites for the new contract rather than MMCs. *Below:* SLS3 was only a week old, service-wise, when photographed at West Croydon on 12th October.

The side-on view gives a better idea of the 'door forward' configuration. Apparently this batch was built to a new length for a DF model. Previously, anything below 10 metres had been the 'wheel forward' design but . . . (see earlier comments about sleep).

LT CONVERSION
Metroline (W) – 8.10.16
Type Change: **Trident & E40H/Enviro400 to Wright New Routemaster**
[LT789-807]

189

D'you get the feeling we haven't had one of these for a while? If so, you'd be right: the New Routemaster programme pretty much ground to a halt between July and September, with only ten new vehicles entering service in that three-month period.

Route 189's conversion was the start of a revival but, blimey oh crikey, it was grindingly slow. Despite the contract renewal date, it had been planned to introduce LTs much earlier, but restrictions on the stand at Brent Cross caused a lengthy delay. Tentative running with older vehicles from Cricklewood's allocation began at the end of August, although a small number from the new batch (no more than eight) had been active on the 16 and 168 since late-June/early July. Four more followed in September, then came the Great Oyster Reader Shortage.

Above: Finally, some of the new batch appeared on the 189. Here's LT798 moving off from its Selfridges stop early on a Saturday morning, before the crowds and the traffic make such shots impossible.

As a continuation of the same batch, four extra vehicles (LT808-811) met a PVR increase on route 16 (another contract renewed on 8th October), so Cricklewood's revised total of NRMs, probably its final total, stood at sixty-eight.

Thanks to the delays, we were able to enjoy the Enviro hybrids for much longer than expected (you have to put a positive spin on it).

Below: TEH1459 is from several batches of 'classic' E400Hs delivered to Cricklewood between 2010 and 2013, which formed a common-user pool for the central area routes. Beatles fans will immediately recognise the pedestrian crossing outside Abbey Road studios. And oh look . . . some workmen have left a pile of crap at the roadside to create an authentic London ambience for the tourists.

LT CONVERSION
Arriva LN (SF)
Type Change: **Volvo B5LH/Eclipse Gemini to Wright New Routemaster**
[LT812-844]

253

You wait ages for an LT conversion, then three come along at once . . . well, two in September/October, which would have been three but for more delays, this time to route 21's elevation.

It's hard to say how late the 253 was, because I don't recall anyone announcing a target date. So let's stick to what happened: The first bus out was LT525, borrowed from the route 73 allocation on September 1st. It was followed by LT356 on the 5th, then various others one at a time – a good way to test a new type in the rough and tumble of daily operation while simultaneously training drivers.

The new vehicles (all thirty-two of them) had to be stored at the Edmonton compound because of the G.O.R.S., so the introduction of the first new bus was delayed until 14th October. LT813 appeared in the morning peak on route 73, two of the older allocation worked the 253.

Other new vehicles appeared at a gradual pace in ones and twos, mostly on the 73, but then it all ground to a halt again. By Christmas, six of the batch were still missing.

Above: The intermittent LT839 ventures out on the 253. This is the first stop after Euston bus station in Eversholt Street.

As it can be quite boring waiting for a bus (never mind thirty of them), let's round off the new vehicles in September/October with the modest type change of the P13.

Another batch of single-deck MMCs appeared in a great rush on the actual day of the new contract (you see, it can be done) and thereafter worked the route alongside 2014-built 'classic' E200s of varying but not dissimilar length.

However, the picture shows a quite interesting 8054 navigating the Tulse Hill one-way system shortly before its withdrawal (the bus, not Tulse Hill). This 2000-built Dart SLF/Pointer spent its final year almost entirely on the P13 and worked its last day in London on the 1st of May 2015. A solitary bag of rubbish awaits the waste management engineers.

Contract Renewal: **Abellio (BC) – 8.10.16**
Partial Type Change: **Dart/SLF/Pointer to E20D 9.7m/Enviro200 MMC [8343-8347]**

P13

Contract Renewals with 'existing fleet'
in September/October

Route 16   Metroline (W) – 8.10.16
Wright New Routemaster   PVR26
(PVR +4 as mentioned earlier)

Route 32   Metroline (W) – 8.10.16
ADL E40H/Enviro400 (ex-189) PVR18

Route 83   Metroline West (ON) – 10.9.16
Volvo B9/Eclipse Gemini   PVR19

Route 107   Metroline (EW) – 8.10.16
Trident/Enviro400   PVR11

Route 117   Metroline (AH) – 3.9.16
Contract Change: from Abellio (TF)
Slated for new vehicles but existing fleet for the time being
E200 Dart 10.2m/Enviro200   PVR 9

Route 132   London Central (BX) - 1.10.16
Eventually vehicles cascaded from route 21 & 63 but, in practice, anything double-deck on the allocation PVR15

Route 137   Arriva LS (BN) – 17.9.16
Wright New Routemaster   PVR31

Route 148   London United (S) - 1.10.16
Wright New Routemaster   PVR25

Route 156   Abellio (QB) – 10.9.16
Trident & E40D/Enviro400   PVR17

Route 160   Arriva LS (DT) – 17.9.16
E40D/Enviro400   PVR12

Route 180   London General (BV) – 1.10.16
Volvo B9/Eclipse Gemini   PVR17

Route 183   London Sovereign (BT) – 3.9.16
Scania OmniCity & Volvo B5LH/Gemini 3 PVR23

Route 203   London United (AV) – 3.9.16
Mercedes Citaro   PVR7

Route 251   London Sovereign (BT) – 3.9.16
E200 Dart/Enviro200   PVR13

Route 276   G-A Docklands (SI) - 17.9.16
E200 Dart/Enviro200   PVR19

Route 279   Arriva LN (E) – 15.10.16
E40D/Enviro400   PVR33

Route 290   Abellio (TF) – 1.10.16
E200 Dart & E20D/Enviro200   PVR7

Route 316   Metroline (W) – 8.10.16
E200 Dart/Enviro200   PVR17

Route 321   London Central (NX) – 8.10.16
Volvo B9/Eclipse Gemini & various   PVR20
In theory, existing vehicles from route 21 when available

Route 346   Blue Triangle (RR) – 1.10.16
Contract Change from Arriva LN (GY)   PVR3
Dart SLF/East Lancs Esteem (ex-route W19)

Route 376   Blue Triangle (RR) – 17.9.16
E200 Dart/Enviro200   PVR8

Route 381   Abellio (WL) – 8.10.16
E40H/Enviro400 ex-3 & 211   PVR19

Route 398   London Sovereign (SO) – 3.9.16
E200 Dart/Enviro200   PVR3

Route 467   Quality Line (EB) – 3.9.16
Trident/Enviro400   PVR2

Route D3   Stagecoach EL (WH) – 17.9.16
E200 Dart/Enviro200   PVR14

Route D7   Docklands (SI) – 17.9.16
Volvo B9/Eclipse Gemini   PVR13

Route H9/10   London Sovereign (SO) – 3.9.16
E200 Dart/Enviro200   PVR16

Route H11   London Sovereign (SO) – 3.9.16
E200 Dart/Enviro200   PVR7

Route P12   London Central (PM) - 8.10.16
E20D/Enviro200   PVR15

Route W3   Arriva LN (WN) – 15.10.16
E40D/Enviro400   PVR23

And if a dozen contracts with new vehicles and thirty with existing fleet isn't enough for you, twelve school routes were also renewed in this two-month period. Unfortunately, space does not permit a full listing, nor does my interest in them.

However, there is room for a photo - a route plucked at random from the list above: The 107 is now worked by early Enviro400s cascaded north to Edgware as a result of LT conversions in the deep south (Cricklewood and Holloway).

Right: From an even earlier period, VPL203 arrives at Edgware bus station. After this photo was taken in 2012, the bus transferred from the local garage to Willesden and worked there until its withdrawal in 2014.

Quite Interesting 2

SOMETIMES I think there should be a section called *Very Interesting* to cover subjects like this. Arriva's HV64 was painted 'platinum' in September to acknowledge the Platinum Award to the company's 1,000 employees who give to various charities through the monthly payroll.

Note also the Routemaster reg, WLT664, and RM/NRM brown wheel paint. A proper job, as they say.

HV64 began life as one of thirty-seven EC spec vehicles that completed the conversion of route 73 to hybrid operation in 2012. After the LTs arrived, it transferred to Palmers Green (August 2015) and has since worked all the double-deck routes there, including the 102.

Most days, though, you're more likely to find it on the 141.

Below: WVL440 was one of the small number of former-route 12 Volvos that *weren't* sprayed around south London after the LT conversion. However, it finally succumbed to the fleet manager's pen at the end of July when it moved to Stockwell and appeared on all the double-deck numbers there, including the 88. It remained for barely four weeks before moving further west to Merton and making a start on another set, although mostly working the newly-acquired 57.

That's what it's doing here in September, showing off both a 'Big T' ad and a Camberwell garage code.

Top of page: The Gemini 2DLs delivered to First Centrewest in 2009 – WN35001-4, sometimes called Merchant Navys because of their numbering – have remained on Tower Transit's books and enjoyed a mid-life refurbishment in 2016. Although the First Group blue poles remain, the new seat moquette is Tower's own. Originally delivered for comparative trials on route 328 alongside early Wright hybrids (all withdrawn from London), the quartet can now be found mostly on the 266. Interior trim aside, they are identical in almost every respect to the DW2XX batch built for Arriva. WN35004 rests between journeys at Hammersmith's lower bus station.

Staying with bus stations, the revamped West Croydon finally opened on Saturday, 8th October, which was stretching "summer 2016" to its limit. However, it was worth the wait because this is a classy conversion, obviously designed by someone who knows what they're doing Complementing the rustic effect of the seating and the real brick, there's some attractive planting, if you're into the herbaceous.

What you cannot hear, because this is not an audio book, is the classical music playing in the background to dissuade young people from congregating, as tried and found effective at several Underground stations. De yoof hate de classics.

Above: As 2002-built vehicles bite the dust in ever-increasing numbers, whither WVL1? A lifelong Stockwell bus, Go-Ahead's first Gemini was originally one of a batch of twenty-seven ordered for a route 345 contract renewal. When the 345 converted to Enviro400s in 2009, half the batch transferred to Putney, but the first thirteen remained and have since been constant performers on the 333, especially as newer kit progressively pushed them off the 11, 87 and 88. The clock is now ticking fast and time is likely to run out for WVL1 and its Gemini group when the 333 transfers to Arriva in January 2017.

Below: In case anyone imagines otherwise, there is no 'plan' for *Quite Interesting* when the year begins. I simply photograph whatever floats past me that looks . . . well, wrong. Then there's the stuff that's intrinsically interesting because of its age or history. This is from the former category – the first time I've seen a route 106 Gemini on any other Ash Grove route. Having said that, there aren't many to choose from. HAs on the 106 are commonplace and VLWs still appear on the 78, but a Gemini on the 78? Fairly rare, although I have seen another since.

DW522 pauses at the Humphrey Road stop opposite OKR Tesco, where routes 168 and 415 have their stands. The lack of proper blinds reinforces the impression of wrong-ness.

LED illumination is universal in modern bus design and some older types have been retro-fitted with the technology (e.g. Merton's PVLs and Sutton's DOEs).

West Ham's Routemasters have re-emerged from their refurbishment with internal LEDs disguised as light bulbs, and there have been a number of Christmas period embellishments to side panel ads on the regular fleet, like 2016's Paco Rabanne and Coach.

Right: Brigit's Afternoon Tea bus adopts a different approach by using LEDs as full-on decoration. And very striking they are too, especially after dark. This is RM909 approaching Tottenham Court Road station at dusk.

Bottom of page: Continuing the LED theme, refurbishments began in the summer on Sutton's Optare double-decks, the backbone of routes 93, 151 & 213. Nos 1-9 disappeared for a considerable time and were eventually spotted at Plaxton's premises in Sheffield

They returned in all-red, naturally, and with the interiors brightened up by NRM-style circular LED clusters. The new seat moquette is Go-Ahead's standard blue, with coloured dots, and the same, comfortable level of padding has been maintained. DOE2 waits between journeys at Kingston's Fairfield bus station.

Not a million miles away (about ten yards, in fact) you will find brand-new Gemini 3s working the Kingston University trips. Two of the regular London fleet, VH45201-2, were diverted to the KU job until more dedicated vehicles arrived. Those that have turned up are 11.4 metre double-doored monsters in a new shade of paint described as 'cool grey'. The university contract is operated by United Motorcoaches, a subsidiary of RATP-Dev based at the former Twickenham bus depot (code NC). *Above:* VH45209, continuing the number sequence of RATP's Volvo hybrid variants, restarts on its way to Seething Wells.

The limited stop KU1 journey begins at East Putney station (District Line) and then more-or-less follows route 85 in the southbound direction, including the detour via the world-famous Roehampton Asda. The new buses have seats for 77 including . . . wait for it . . . three tip-ups (praise the Lord, something else to rattle on about).

Below: The 436 was re-routed from 19th November to run to Battersea Park instead of Paddington, following the 156 and 344 from Vauxhall to serve the major redevelopment along the south bank of the river.

Some might think this a little premature as the entire eastern end of Battersea Park Road remains a gigantic building site that looks years away from the arrival of people needing all-day buses. Whatever, here's one of the 436's dedicated hybrids, WHV8, crossing the railway tracks leading to Stewarts Lane depot, just before the penultimate stop outside Battersea Dogs' Home . . .

. . . whose post now has an extra e-plate at the top. What the name panel doesn't show is any apostrophes. Without them, dogs and cats become nouns again, home becomes a verb, and the stop tells passers-by that dogs and cats home . . . like pigeons. Sort it out, TfL.

Above: Although double-deck substitutions on the X26 are quite common, you don't see many photos of them. This raises the rarity to a higher notch because it's a Hounslow Enviro400 working the express route rather than one of Quality Line's DDs.

ADE45 went on loan to Epsom garage in October and appeared on all manner of local routes from the 15th. Journeys on the X26 were sporadic, but they were still happening as New Year approached. This is the roundabout outside Hatton Cross station, at the end of the Heathrow free bus area.

Below: This photo was taken in December to illustrate a September event. Why? Because it was so far under the radar that I failed to notice (until December) that LT62 had gone back to Stockwell and, more to the point, route 11. Readers with long memories will recall page 14 and the bus's return to service on Camberwell routes after a two-and-a-half year holiday in Northern Ireland. I've heard of returning to the scene of former triumphs, but never to the scene of former disasters.

Above: Both of these appear in the Miscellaneous Vehicles table at the back of the book as one is a demonstrator and one used to be a demonstrator. WS65 is a 10.2 metre StreetLite in 'door forward' configuration that went first to New Cross for trials of its Mercedes engine on route 108. After moving to Camberwell, it appeared on the P5 for about a month but then became a regular on the 360. Here it's pulling away from the Elephant & Castle Station stop, although you need local knowledge to find the Thameslink platforms hidden in the darkest recesses of the shopping centre.

Below: Meanwhile, at the Bakerloo Line entrance . . . After its training stint at Mandela Way, WHV111 joined the brand-new Gemini 3s on route 1 and was still there at Christmas. It's an interim Gemini 3 arrangement, with extra light clusters and the shallower, weight-saving windows on the top deck. The lower deck saloon has been re-trimmed in Go-Ahead's current moquette (unlike the two diesel demonstrators at Croydon - WVL509 & 510). Otherwise, the layout is similar to the latest Volvo B5/Gemini, with staggered height rear seats over the wheel arches.

Vinyl Variations 2

Above: You would normally expect a rash of perfume and after-shave ads as Christmas approaches, but this one for Daisy fragrances appeared in July. They're fifty-four quid a pop in Debenham's, although the illustrations on the side of LT534 suggest they come in very big bottles.

Right & Below: We had Magnum adverts in 2015 but this was for a new double chocolate indulgence in the summer, inviting us to 'release the beast'. I can think of a completely different meaning for that. As for 'dare to go double' . . . On the side of the many LTs carrying the ad, the eyes of a leopard followed you . . . or was it the eyes of a woman . . . or did I imagine the whole thing?
  This is LT456 on the stand of route 453 at Marylebone.

Above: There was only one of these and I only saw it once. 9527 stands at Vauxhall promoting the Europa Park resort near Stuttgart in Germany. I can tell you no more, as I have only been to Stuttgart once and that was thirty years ago.

Left: This one didn't work for me; for a start, white text on a nearly-white background made it hard to read (especially for old people) and the design, for want of a better word, added nothing to the message. LT397, American Airlines, flying past the Bank of England.

Below: The 2016 Coco-Cola design appeared on a multitude of LTs for much of the year. I presume the children who concocted this mess thought it looked really cool, and I further presume that none of the grown-ups in the marketing agency had the wit to *tell* them it was a mess. LT98, turning into Bayswater Road, looks even worse against the verdant July lushness of Hyde Park.

I realise the reaction to all of these is entirely subjective (beauty in the eye of the beholder, *et cetera*), but I thought this looked amazing – perhaps the first dark blue advert on a red bus to work effectively. Why? Because there's a little bit of red in the design, so it doesn't matter if some of the bus colour pokes through. Why did no-one think of that before? As it's so lovely, I'm showing you both sides, as displayed by LT162 at Hammersmith and LT737 near Oxford Circus. And what is it? Tommy Hilfiger again, now producing chic for chicks.

Above: On-line fashion retailer Zalando came up with this slightly-confused concoction, but that was the clever part: You had to read the words to figure out what it was . . . if you were a bloke. The single word 'shop' would have been enough to grab the attention of most women. For those who couldn't care less, this is LT171 waiting time at Hammersmith.

Below: From the autumn, half-a-dozen LTs began supporting Man City by displaying the colours worn by the team in Champions League away games. By pure chance, the orange and mauve were similar to the wrapper of a Cadbury's 'double Decker' bar, allowing two plugs for the price of one. LT374 begins a route 55 journey from the Holles Street stop near Oxford Circus.

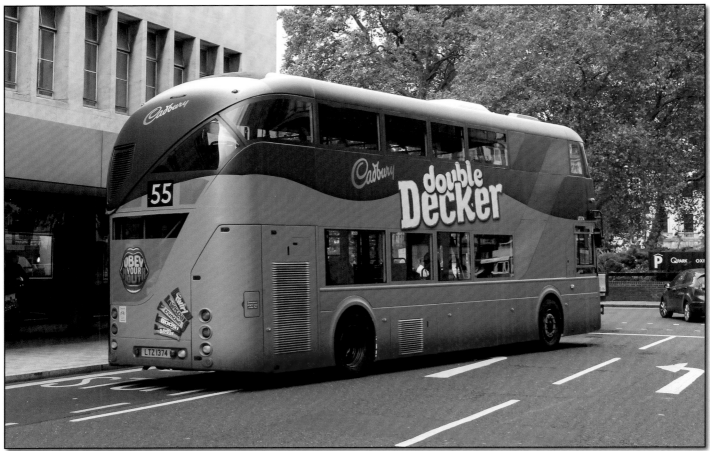

Above: A revised version of the London General livery applied to LT60 appeared on LT50 to coincide with the Stockwell open day on 15th October. Here's the bus bathed in autumn gold at Vauxhall a few days later, working the 88. As we've noticed many times before, LTs look so much better with a full skirt at the front, rather then the silly Pudsey Bear effect of the sloping panel. Yes, I know this isn't an advert. Yes, I know it isn't vinyl.

Below: As a reminder that not all vinyl wraps appeared on LTs in the second half of the year any more than the first, here's the Austrian ski resort of Zillertal promoting its 500 kilometres of pistes on the sides of Tottenham's DW440 in October. Is skiing very big in Tottenham?

Above: The 2016 Poppy design was exactly the same as the 2015 Poppy Design and was applied to a similar mix of bus types – ten vehicles in all. One of the LTs, Bow's LT239, was painted white as a background to the poppies, but this one is clearly an all-over vinyl – LT455 on route 12 at Trafalgar Square.

Below: The Spotify music streaming service appeared in this minimalist form in October – another clever ploy to encourage people to Google and discover more. I did, and discovered you can get music for free. Well, well, who knew?

Above: A few editions back, I suggested a Lego bus might make another bonkers project for the mayor to pursue. Well, nearly . . . Around half-a-dozen NRMs were commandeered to promote the new Lego store from the beginning of November and continued in this guise for . . . um, ages. I saw one when I attempted to do my Christmas shopping two days before Christmas. This, however, is from late autumn - hence the harsh, low sunlight. Clapton's LT219 at Piccadilly Circus on the 38.

Below: Weather-wise, most of late autumn and December was like this - grey. LT64 tries to brighten the mood with its plethora of colours to promote Indonesia on the approach to Ludgate Circus (and on the rest of the route, obviously).

Above: Kate Spade, fashionista of New York, now has branches in central London and a spate of Kates advertised the fact in late autumn on various NRMs. This is LT298 on route 453 outside the Old Kent Road Tesco. The ad probably made more of an impression when the bus was trundling up and down Regent Street.

Below: This one was referred to as 'Aussie Skincare' but appears to be advertising a hair conditioner. Clearly the Australian beauty industry has come a long way since the immortal line: "And Bruce here is in charge of the sheep dip."

Above: In November and December, five LTs carried holiday ads for Egypt, featuring Giza in the Nile Valley (where you can find half-a-dozen assorted pyramids and the Great Sphinx) and variations on the Red Sea Riviera. Holloway's LT762 engages in a spot of pyramid-selling outside Holborn tube station.

Below: Vinyl on vinyl - The Stones' first studio album for more than a decade appeared on only one all-over wrap, on Arriva's LT539. I'd have given them a whole lot more as a reward for stamina alone. I cashed a cheque for Mick Jagger in 1975 . . . you know.

Above: I had to look this up, as staring at it in the street made no sense at all. Bumble is a dating app "known for empowering women" and this is how it works: If 'a chap' receives a text message via Bumble from 'a lady', he has to reply within a certain time, otherwise the family jewels could be ostracised. There may be more to it than that, but I can't figure out what it is. Abellio's 9541 in Bressenden Place.

Below: The 2016 end-of-year ads for YouTube looked remarkably similar to the 2015 end-of-year ads for YouTube and equally bland. Don't get me wrong: I love YT and probably spend more time sifting through its music and old films than watching conventional telly these days, but its advertising is . . . well, dull. This is LT695 on the 211, pausing to admire the Christmas decs in Duke of York Square. Ho, ho, ho.

FOLLOWING a 'bus-heavy' October for new vehicles entering service, November continued in similar vein as the re-equipment of eight more routes and a continued clearing of the backlog combined to produce another three-figure number.

The 63 and 363 are linked routes that overlap between Elephant & Castle and the Forest Hill Tavern stop in Honor Oak. The northern and southern extensions are E&C-King's Cross (63) and Honor Oak-Crystal Palace (363). Although a hard core of the 'proper' buses turned out daily, there were frequent and numerous substitutions between routes – a practice that continued as soon as new batch vehicles became available.

Officially, the 63 will henceforth be MHV-operated, while the 363 has its dedicated batch of Enviro MMCs. However, day to day . . .

Above: The first picture shows the last of the 31-strong Gemini 2 batch (WVL303-333) delivered against the most recent contract renewal in 2009. A huge banner emblazoned with a 1970s photograph of the Royal Family looked out across the Thames at Blackfriars from Sea Containers House for the duration of the 2012 Olympics. I never did find out why.

Below: Showing an MHV on the 63 is far too obvious, so here's one on the 37. Why? Because many of the new intake began their London careers on either the night route or the daytime 37. I suppose the thinking was that

they'd cause less chaos if they broke down between Peckham and Putney rather than on Blackfriars Bridge or outside King's Cross station. MHV35 coasts down Putney Hill after setting off from the Green Man on its second day in service. You will note that this batch has lost the window at the foot of the stairs to allow a full T-panel to be fitted (see MHV20 opposite for comparison).

Opposite page top: For lovers of the esoteric, here's MHV34, also on its second day in service, replacing rails at Purley station. The line from here to Redhill was shut for 'improvement works' on the weekend of 26th/27th November and Go-Ahead provided a selection of alternative transport from its south London garages. As well as the Peckham Evoseti, Putney sent along WHV36 & WVL508, while E144 drove down from Merton.

In the background is WVL272, once of Bexleyheath but now part of the Commercial Services fleet. As you can see from the side banner, it had latterly been deployed on the Vauxhall-Battersea workers' shuttles.

Contract Renewal: London Central (PM) – 12.11.16
Type Change: Volvo B9TL/Eclipse Gemini to
Volvo B5LH/MCV EvoSeti   [MHV21-55]

63

Some Conclusions

AS the MCV EvoSeti body is 'new for 2016' in London, here are my thoughts after travelling in a fair number and taking a close look.

Despite initial reservations, I'd say Go-Ahead is onto a winner with the Pharoah Volvo. Yes, it is a bit slab-like, but the curved edges combined with the shape of the light clusters is a pleasing combination that does 'grow on you'. (I offer the English Electric Class 50s as a railway parallel. Everyone thought they looked terrible at first but grew to love them.)

Where the EvoSeti-bodied Volvo B5 really scores is in the important area of price, something that may give UK manufacturers pause for thought. Although the prices paid by individual operators remain highly confidential, there is said to be a significant gap between the foreign-bodied Volvo B5 hybrid and the domestically-produced vehicle. If so, we shall be seeing many more of this combination on the city's streets. As things stand, Tower Transit has ordered fifty-odd for delivery in 2017, for both east and west London, and they won't be the last.

Having said all that, I should sound the cautionary note that you get what you pay for. The workmanship is a little clumsy in places, then there's the mastic sealant around some of the interior panels that gives the impression of sitting in a bath. These are small quibbles, though, for something that is undeniably good value, remarkably cheerful, and quite handsome in the right light.

Contract Renewal: London Central (Q) – 12.11.16
Type Change: Volvo B7TL/President to
ADL E40H/Enviro400 MMC   [EH61-73]

363

Above: The old 363 was mostly all-PVL, but with interlopers from the 63's Gemini collection. This is PVL335 approaching journey's end at Crystal Palace in the autumn of 2014. Latterly, Peckham's allocation was PVL329-342 and all were withdrawn by November the 9th, thanks to a speedy introduction of the new MMCs.

Below: The first couple of Enviros appeared in the week up to 31st October and the last of thirteen, EH70, was on the road by November 15th. A couple of them also made it to Putney Heath in the first fortnight on the 37. However, here's the correct bus on the correct route – EH71 pulling away from the aforementioned Forest Hill Tavern stop in Honor Oak. The Yorkshire number plates are intriguing as they suggest another batch built in Scarborough.

Contract Renewal: London General (AF) – 19.11.16
Type Change: Volvo B7TL/Eclipse Gemini to
ADL E40H/Enviro400 MMC   [EH74-112]

14

Some might say the conversion of Putney garage to full hybrid is long overdue, but a number of measures had already been put in place to reduce diesel pollution in the High Street. The early Volvo B7s, for instance, had their exhaust traps modified around the time they were refurbished to reduce both CO_2 and particulate emissions.

Readers will also recall that the hybrids ordered for the route 22 contract renewal in 2012 were diverted to the 14 and 74 because those routes traverse the High Street and the 22 does not. The latest round of new contracts provided the perfect opportunity to complete the job, using both Volvo B5 and ADL diesel-electric variants.

Above: First, though, the old guard, represented by WVL29 at the Royal Academy stop in Piccadilly. As well as the fourteen vehicles transferred from Stockwell, Putney received a new batch of its own in 2002, WVL28-71, for the 74 and 85. The final large batch, WVL160-211, arrived in south-west London in 2005 and converted routes 14 and 22 from

Routemaster to low-floor operation. Since then, they've all worked as one giant common-user pool, which is now nearing the end of its useful life in London terms.

As you may have read earlier, Go-Ahead deliberately ordered batches of both Volvo and ADL chassis vehicle for the Putney upgrades, to allow another "nose to nose" comparison under different operating conditons. The common-user arrangement ensured that both types appeared on all the double-deck routes from Day One, so . . .

Below: . . . despite their nominal allocation to route 14, many of the Enviros first ran on the 74, partly because it stands in Putney garage at the end of the southbound journey, allowing minor problems to be addressed between trips. This is EH75, backlit by a low winter sun at Marble Arch on December the 14th. It will come as no surprise that the day after this photo was taken, the bus resurfaced on route 337.

| 74 | Contract Renewals: London General (AF) – 19.11.16
Type Change: Volvo B7TL & B9TL/Eclipse Gemini to
Volvo B5LH/Gemini   [WHV112-142 & 158-167] | 430 |

Above: As well as the ten hybrids, thirteen Euro 5 diesel Geminis (WVL496-508) were ordered for route 22 in 2012 and also ended up mostly on the 'High Street routes', so here we have WVL504 working the 74 at South Kensington. The latest Gemini 3s were ordered against the renewals of both the 74 and 430. However . . .

Below: Common-user rools OK, so this batch of new kit also appeared from the start on all of Putney's double-deck numbers. Here, then, is an unremarkable working by WHV131 on the 22 only a few days after entering service. Thanks to a clear run from Piccadilly, the bus is having to wait time at the Knightsbridge station stop – a common sight on many central area routes on Saturday mornings before the traffic builds up.

Contract Change: Abellio (BC) to Arriva LS (N) – 12.11.16
Type Change: Volvo B7TL 10.6m/Eclipse Gemini to Trident/Enviro400 [ex-route 133]

157

Travel London's flirtation with Wright-bodied vehicles did not continue when Abellio took over the operation (strictly speaking, Ned Railways trading as Abellio), so the first orders totalling seventy-three 10.6 metre buses have not been added to – no Gemini 2s, no Gemini 3s.
Above: Here, then, a type we can add to the endangered list, represented by 9072 at the Crystal Palace end of the 157.
  Thirteen vehicles (9021-33, all eleven years old) were stood down temporarily after the contract loss but most resurfaced at other Abellio depots. 9072 has since moved on to Walworth.

Cascading vehicles from route 133 for this acquisition wasn't as easy as it sounds, not least because the 133 wasn't due new buses (Enviro 400H Citys) until 2017. However, there are clues earlier in the book: Stamford Hill hybrids transferring to Brixton, allowing Brixton DWs to move to Norwood for the 133, releasing the dedicated Enviros more than a month early. *Below:* So here we have a weather-stained T190 between the Carshalton Ponds on December the 8th. In the foreground is the mis-named Ann Boleyn's Well. In the background, the ducks are suffering a seagull invasion. Still, makes a change from pigeons.

November and December also produced a number of quite interesting single-deck conversions to new vehicles - not all of which were MMCs. They were so interesting, in fact, that they get rather more space than usual.

Although the new kit was something different, route 39 was a straightforward changeover at renewal, producing more StreetLites in south London after their successful introduction on Merton's 219.

Above: The old was more likely than not a Transbus Dart Pointer from late-2002, like LDP 212 waiting time on the stand at Putney Bridge. The batch (LDP211-221, minus one stray) were progressively withdrawn as new vehicles arrived at Plough Lane garage.

Below: A brand-new WS69 at the other end of the route – Grant Road, Clapham Junction – on November the 24th. Another of the old Pointers stands alongside. Three new vehicles appeared soon after the contract date, but no more had entered service by Christmas (refer to the outstanding list on page 130).

Contract Renewal: London General (PL) – 19.11.16
Type Change: Dart SLF/Pointer to StreetLite DF 10.8m [WS66-73]

39

The old W19 contract had been operated by Go-Ahead for ten years, initially from Silvertown (G-A Docklands). At the last renewal in 2011, it moved to the Blue Triangle depot at Rainham and transferred again when River Road received its main allocation in July.

It had long been rumoured that Hackney CT would build a new depot on the site of Walthamstow Stadium – a prediction that proved inaccurate by about two hundred yards. *Above:* You can't actually take this photo because of the angle of the footbridge and the position of lamp posts, but a stitched-together panorama shows the relative position of the new site to the stadium façade.

This former patch of waste ground has been concreted over and fenced to provide a maintenance facility and bus wash and there's enough room to park many of Hackney's minibus fleet (the white vehicles) alongside. It's a bit messy, but probably easier than arm-wrestling Arriva for extra space at Ash Grove.

Contract Change: Blue Triangle (RR) to CT Plus (AW) – 26.11.16
Type Change: Dart SLF/Evolution & others to ADL E20D 9.6m/Enviro200 [1221-1237]

W19

Two routes will initially be based here – the newly-acquired W19, and the 385 – although at PVR 1 (see last year's *RAO*) the 385 won't present much of a challenge. Eight of the new E200s (built to the 'classic' pattern externally) appeared on the first day – 1221-25/1228/1232 (not shown on Countdown/LVF) & 1237.

Left: The 'invisible' 1232 shows off its classic front-end at Walthamstow bus station on the first morning in real brass monkey weather. The blurred lettering of the blind is caused by condensation behind the glass.

All seventeen new buses were in service by the Monday afternoon peak, with one having worked the off-peak 385, a route whose northbound journey begins close to the new depot at the Crooked Billet Sainsbury's.

Above: Here's a major development, though: The vehicles have been built with the same interior scheme as ADL's Enviro400H City which, you will recall, CT ordered for its takeover of route 26. That means the revised TfL moquette, red resin fittings and bronze poles . . . all of which call for non-standard component orders to be placed, perhaps at extra cost. Somebody must have really wanted this.

Contract Change: London General (A) to Quality Line (EB) – 3.12.16
Type Change: Dart/Esteem & various Enviro200s to
Mercedes Citaro-K 10.6m   [MCS01-09]

413

Morden 413

The 413 runs to Bushey Road in Sutton and has its stand alongside the Go-Ahead garage. London General had worked the route since 2001 after winning it from Quality Line. Dart Pointers (LDPs) were the early G-A motive power but, latterly, it was a mix of SE and SOE – in other words, Darts with different bodies. *Below:* From a more recent period, this is SE170, an E20D from the 2011 intake.

Readers of earlier editions will recall the meanderings of Mercedes' 10.6 metre Euro-6 demonstrator. One of its ports of call in the past three years was Epsom Buses, a trial that resulted in an order for nine similar vehicles when Quality Line won back the 413 contract. You don't need me to tell you how lovely these buses are and how comfortable they are to ride on. And they don't rattle.

Above: MCS03 at the Stonecot Hill stop in North Cheam, soon after emerging from the Hail & Ride section into a brief spell of sunshine.

Opposite page bottom: In the first week, cursed by rubbish weather again, MCS04 pulls away from West Sutton station, the one and only fixed stop in the H&R.

Opposite page top: The interiors are finished in QL's red moquette. Note the double jump-seat by the front doors rather than the single version on earlier models. At the back, there is a standard theatre style layout – in other words, the short Citaro does not have the transverse seats of the 12 metre bus. Above the legal notices on the cab bulkhead, there's a personal message from QL's Managing Director, Steve Whiteway.

The demonstrator – BU13 ZVE – has given up the nomadic life and joined the Epsom fleet as MCS10 . . . probably. Although intended as a back-up to the nine new buses on the 413, it worked for much of December on the 411 alongside the equally one-off HOV1 and OC1.

Sutton Town Centre 413

Contract Change: Abellio (BC) to London General (C) – 3.12.16
Type Change: Various Dart & E200 to various E200
[existing fleet]

152

Despite the change of operator, the 152's replacement vehicles were only new to the route. But they were as varied a bunch as those they replaced - a gathering of displaced E200 variants from such places as Silvertown (following the double-decking of route D8), New Cross (after the influx of refurbised Citaros to the 108) and Camberwell (rendered redundant by the 42's double-decking).

Above: One of Abellio's long-serving Pointers, 8473, navigates the roundabout in front of The Fountain in New Malden on its way to the nearby stand. After the changeover, the 2006-built vehicles were stood down; the more recent E200s replaced older vehicles on other Beddington routes, like the 433, 455 and P13.

Below: H20 is one of the Hounslow 'H's rather than the Harrow ones and runs a circuitous circuit from the Civic Centre to the Twickenham Tesco's, usually referred to as Ivybridge. This four-mile journey at a 12-minute frequency produces a vehicle requirement of six - hence seven new buses to replace seven old ones.

As far as I can tell, the new MMCs are perfectly ordinary stubby jobs with a single door and an emergency exit. Demonstrating the point is 8155, heading for the last stop alongside Tesco's car park, only a stone's throw from the world-famous Twickenham rugby stadium.

Contract Renewal: Abellio (TF) – 19.11.16
Type Change: Dart SLF/Pointer to
ADL E20D 8.9m/Enviro200 MMC [8155-8161]

H20

LT CONVERSION
Contract Renewal: London Central (NX) - 8.10.16
Type Change: Volvo B9/Eclipse Gemini & others to Wright New Routemaster
[LT845-874]

21

This was another 'work in progress' as the year drew to a close, but it should arguably have happened in October. Only ten vehicles had entered service by 31st December (LT846/9/51/4/7/9/62/5-7) with the other twenty parked at West Ham until Oyster readers were forthcoming.

The last contract renewal in October 2009 was achieved with a dedicated pool of diesel Volvos - WVL274-302 - but in recent years the allocation had become mixed with the similar Volvo batch for route 171 and other types at New Cross.

Here's two of the new intake braving the winter weather:
Above: LT865 sparkling in the murk outside the Royal Exchange. Because of a long-term lane closure at Moorgate, the southbound 21 was diverted via Eldon Street, London Wall and Old Broad Street, regaining line of route at Bank after emerging from Threadneedle Street.
Below: LT862 'straight out of the box' on the last day of the year at the London Bridge Station stop. The sharp-eyed will have noticed the continued absence of opening windows on both vehicles.

Contract Renewal: Abellio (WS) – 31.12.16
Type Change: Dart SLF/Pointer to
ADL E20D 8.9m/Enviro200 MMC [8162-8165]

U9

The final new contract of 2016 fell due on the 31st December but no new buses appeared, although the four replacement MMCs had been delivered. Until they venture out in the New Year (future tense to maintain the time conceit), route U9 will have to soldier on with its collection of Dart Pointers, like 8113 in Uxbridge High Street.

And talking of Uxbridge . . . if you're pining for the Metroline DELs that should have entered service on route 487 but didn't . . . here's one of them working from Uxbridge garage. All except one trickled out on the garage's local routes - mostly U2 and U3 but also 331 - in the latter half of the year. *Below:* DEL2157 completes its journey at Heathrow Central bus station on a particularly dank day.

Contract Renewals with 'existing fleet'
in November/December

Route 38   Arriva LN (CT) – 12.11.16
Wright New Routemaster   PVR52 [-7]

Route 221   Arriva LN (WN) – 5.11.16
DB300/Gemini 2DL (ex-242 eventually)   PVR23

Route 313   Arriva LN (E) – 5.11.16
E20D 10.8m/Enviro200   PVR8

Route 436   London Central (NX) – 19.11.16
Volvo B5LH/Gemini 2 & ADL E40H/Enviro400
                    PVR21 [+1]

Route U7   Abellio (WS) – 19.11.16
E200 Dart 10.2m/Enviro200   PVR5

AND so to The Tables . . . which are fairly heavyweight compared to some previous years and would have been even more heavyweight if every vehicle linked to new contracts and LT conversions had entered service by the 31st of December as planned. Instead, just shy of 100, mostly double-decks, remained outstanding as the year drew to a close.

The often-quoted reason for the delays was a lack of Oyster readers and ticket machines, which are installed as a combined unit and are generally donated by withdrawn vehicles.

Obviously new buses have to enter service before old ones can be stood down and their equipment recovered, and the gap between those two events is meant to be covered by an equipment float. That float no longer exists, we are told, hence the problem.

NRMs present an extra challenge because they need four Oyster readers - one in the traditional position with a ticket machine and three more on the poles behind the centre and rear doors. The 'stand-alones' are colour-keyed to the rest of the interior and therefore specific to LTs, so a stock of new units is needed for each batch of vehicles.

As with all complex situations, there is "more to it than that", but I hope the explanation sheds some light on why so many buses are delayed.

Contract Extensions in 2016

Let us continue with what *did* happen in the twelve-month period: All these are two-year extensions under the Quality Incentive scheme, effective from the dates shown. In other words, the tendering process will award new contracts on corresponding dates in 2018. For ease of access they're listed in route order.

Route	Date	Operator	Code
9	03/09/2016	Ldn United	V
12	05/11/2016	Ldn Central	Q
30	25/06/2016	Tower	LI
31	30/04/2016	Tower	AS
61	03/12/2016	Selkent	TB
68	02/04/2016	Ldn Central	Q
73	03/09/2016	Arriva LN	SF
79	26/11/2016	Metroline	PA
95	30/04/2016	Metroline West	G
99	23/01/2016	Selkent	PD
105	02/07/2016	Metroline	PA
118	06/02/2016	Ldn General	AL
144	15/10/2016	Arriva LN	WN
169	26/03/2016	Stagecoach EL	BK
171	30/04/2016	Ldn Central	NX
172	19/03/2016	Abellio	WL
178	23/01/2016	Selkent	TL
181	19/03/2016	Metrobus	MB
193	01/10/2016	Blue Triangle	BE
196	07/05/2016	Ldn General	SW
209	20/08/2016	Metroline	AH
223	15/10/2016	Metroline West	ON
224	15/10/2016	Metroline West	ON
241	07/05/2016	Stagecoach EL	WH
244	23/01/2016	Ldn General	BV
247	26/03/2016	Stagecoach EL	NS
258	06/02/2016	Arriva LN	GR
269	23/01/2016	Selkent	TB
274	25/06/2016	Metroline	KC
287	26/03/2016	Stagecoach EL	RM
291	23/01/2016	Selkent	PD
299	06/02/2016	Ldn General	NP
330	07/05/2016	Stagecoach EL	WH
337	28/05/2016	Ldn General	SW
343	06/02/2016	Abellio	WL
387	26/03/2016	Stagecoach EL	BK
389	09/04/2016	Ldn General	NP
390	03/09/2016	Metroline	HT
399	09/04/2016	Ldn General	NP
401	23/01/2016	Ldn Central	BX
403	29/10/2016	Arriva	TC
422	23/01/2016	Ldn Central	BX
423	05/03/2016	Ldn United	HH
452	03/12/2016	Abellio	QB
453	19/11/2016	Ldn General	MW
468	02/04/2016	Ldn Central	Q
474	30/04/2016	Docklands	SI
B11	23/01/2016	Ldn Central	BX
B14	06/02/2016	Metrobus	MB
B16	23/01/2016	Ldn Central	BX
D6	17/09/2016	Docklands	SI
D8	17/09/2016	Docklands	SI
H2	11/06/2016	Arriva LN	GR
H3	11/06/2016	Arriva LN	GR
H12	03/09/2016	Ldn Sovereign	HD
H14	03/09/2016	Ldn Sovereign	SO
H17	03/09/2016	Ldn Sovereign	SO
H22	05/03/2016	Ldn United	HH
H25	19/11/2016	Abellio	TF
H37	05/03/2016	Ldn United	AV
H98	05/03/2016	Ldn United	AV
R9	20/08/2016	Metrobus	MB
W4	06/02/2016	Ldn General	NP
W6	06/02/2016	Arriva LN	EC
X68	02/04/2016	Ldn Central	Q

New Vehicles by Type (numbers into service)

Type	Number	Operator
ADL E20D 8.9m/Enviro200 *	4	Go-Ahead (3) CT Plus (1)
ADL E20D 9.6m/Enviro200 *	17	CT Plus
ADL E20D 10.8m/Enviro200 *	9	Go-Ahead
ADL E20D 8.9m/Enviro200 MMC	52	Abellio (34) Arriva (5) Stagecoach (13)
ADL E20D 9.7m/Enviro200 MMC	14	Abellio (5) Arriva (7) Go-Ahead (2)
ADL E20D 10.8m/Enviro200 MMC	57	Abellio (32) Ldn United (14) Metroline (11)
ADL E40D/Enviro400 *	31	Arriva
ADL E40D/Enviro400 MMC	43	Stagecoach
ADL E40H/Enviro400 MMC	102	Abellio (18) Go-Ahead (46) Stagecoach (38)
ADL E40H/Enviro400 VE	1	Tower
ADL E40H/Enviro400H City	26	Arriva (5) CT Plus (21)
BYD D9UR 12m/Enviro200 EV	44	Go-Ahead
Mercedes Citaro-K 10.6m	9	Quality Line
Volvo B5LH/Enviro400 MMC	21	Stagecoach
Volvo B5LH/Gemini 3	200	Go-Ahead (54) Metroline (73) RATP (48) Tower (25)
Volvo B5LH/MCV EvoSeti	83	Go-Ahead
Volvo B5LH/SRM	4	RATP
Wright StreetLite DF 9.7m	22	Arriva
Wright StreetLite DF 10.8m	3	Go-Ahead
Wright StreetDeck **	9	Arriva
Wright New Routemaster	191	Abellio (46) Arriva (55) Go-Ahead (37) Metroline (53)

* Indicates 'classic' models with old-style body
** StreetDeck chassis with Gemini 3 body

New Vehicles Into Service by Month

Month	Fleet numbers		Type	Operator	Garage	Route	Contract Date	
January	13082-87/97	7	Volvo B5LH/Enviro400 MMC	Selkent	TL	47	23/01/2016	
	DH38503	1	ADL Enviro400 VE	Tower Transit	LI	69	30/04/2016	
	HA14/16-19	5	ADL Enviro400H City	Arriva LN	AE	78	14/11/2015	
	LT650/2/7/9/62	5	Wright New Routemaster	Metroline	W	168		1
	SE276/9/80/2-7	9	ADL E20D 10.8m/Enviro200	Ldn General	AL	164	05/12/2015	
	T301-19/21-5/7	25	ADL E40D/Enviro400	Arriva KT	DT	229/492	23/01/2016	
	WHV81/93/7/8/102/3	6	Volvo B5LH/Gemini 3	Ldn General	AL	155	12/12/2015	
	WHV105-9	5	Volvo B5LH/Gemini 3	Ldn General	A	93	05/12/2015	
		63						
February	13088-96/98/9/100-2	14	Volvo B5LH/Enviro400 MMC	Selkent	TL	47	23/01/2016	
	ENR1-7	7	ADL E20D 9.7m/Enviro200 MMC	Arriva KT	DT	B13	23/01/2016	
	LT664/66-83/5/6	21	Wright New Routemaster	Ldn Central	Q	68		1
	LT691/2/4/5/7-9/700-15	23	Wright New Routemaster	Abellio	QB	3		1
	T320/8/9/30/1	5	ADL E40D/Enviro400	Arriva KT	DT	229/492	23/01/2016	
	WHV110	1	Volvo B5LH/Gemini 3	Ldn General	A	93	05/12/2015	
		71						
March	1220	1	ADL E20D 8.9m/Enviro200	CT Plus	HK	W5	06/02/2016	
	8210-19	10	ADL Enviro200 MMC 8.9m	Abellio	BC	367	19/03/2016	
	8844-59/61-4	20	ADL Enviro200 MMC 10.9m	Abellio	QB	C10	19/03/2016	
	LT651	1	Wright New Routemaster	Metroline	W	168		1
	LT693/6	2	Wright New Routemaster	Abellio	QB	3		1
	LT718/9/23-5/7/8/33/7/8/44	11	Wright New Routemaster	Arriva LS	BN	59		1
	SE288-90	3	ADL E20D 8.9m/Enviro200	Ldn General	MB	162	19/03/2016	
	T326	1	ADL E40D/Enviro400	Arriva KT	DT	229/492	23/01/2016	
	VH38112-7/9/20/1	9	Volvo B5LH/Gemini 3	Tower Transit	AS	328	30/04/2016	
	VH45153-61	9	Volvo B5LH/Gemini 3	Ldn United	S	94		2
		67						
April	8860	1	ADL E20D 10.8m/Enviro200 MMC	Abellio	QB	C10	19/03/2016	
	10309/10/2/3/5/26/8/9/30-32	11	ADL E40D/Enviro400 MMC	Stagecoach EL	BK	62/145	30/04/2016	
	10333/5	2	ADL E40D/Enviro400 MMC	Stagecoach EL	NS	294	30/04/2016	
	EH39-52/4/6-60	20	ADL E40H/Enviro400 MMC	Ldn Central	Q	35/40	30/04/2016	3
	LT684/7-90	5	Wright New Routemaster	Ldn Central	Q	68		1
	LT716/7/20-2/6/9/30 & LT731/2/4-6/9/40-3	18	Wright New Routemaster	Arriva LS	BN	59		1
	MHV2-13/5/6/7/9/20	17	Volvo B5LH/MCV EvoSeti	Ldn Central	Q	35/40	30/04/2016	3
	SE291/2	2	ADL E20D 9.7m/Enviro200 MMC	Ldn Central	Q	P5	30/04/2016	
	VH38118/22-36	16	Volvo B5LH/Gemini 3	Tower Transit	AS	328	30/04/2016	
	VH45162/4/5/6	4	Volvo B5LH/Gemini 3	Ldn United	S	94		2
		96						
May	8138-41	4	ADL E20D 8.9m/Enviro200 MMC	Abellio	TF	481	07/05/2016	
	8142-54	13	ADL E20D 8.9m/Enviro200 MMC	Abellio	WS	E5	28/05/2016	
	8865-73/5	10	ADL E20D 10.8m/Enviro200 MMC	Abellio	WS	E7	28/05/2016	
	10308/11/4/6-25/7	14	ADL E40D/Enviro400 MMC	Stagecoach EL	BK	62/145	30/04/2016	
	10334/6-42/4-6	11	ADL E40D/Enviro400 MMC	Stagecoach EL	NS	294	30/04/2016	
	EH53/5	2	ADL E40H/Enviro400 MMC	Ldn Central	Q	35/40	30/04/2016	3
	LT745-51/3-65	20	Wright New Routemaster	Metroline	HT	91		1
	LT770/1/3	3	Wright New Routemaster	Abellio	QB	211		1
	MHV1/14/8	3	Volvo B5LH/MCV EvoSeti	Ldn Central	Q	35/40	30/04/2016	3
	ST812	1	Wright New Routemaster 10.2m	Metroline	HT	91		4
	VH45163	1	Volvo B5LH/Gemini 3	Ldn United	S	94		2
	VH45167/8	2	Volvo B5LH/Gemini 3	Ldn United	TV	85	02/07/2016	
		84						
June	2501-12/4/6	14	ADL Enviro400H City	CT Plus	HK	26	27/02/2016	5
	8874	1	ADL E20D 10.8m/Enviro200 MMC	Abellio	WS	E7	28/05/2016	
	10343/7	2	ADL E40D/Enviro400 MMC	Stagecoach EL	NS	294	30/04/2016	
	EN34-8	5	ADL E20D 8.9m/Enviro200 MMC	Arriva LN	E	377	09/07/2016	
	LT665	1	Wright New Routemaster	Ldn Central	Q	68		1
	LT752/66	2	Wright New Routemaster	Metroline	HT	91		1
	LT767/96/7	3	Wright New Routemaster	Metroline	W	189		1
	LT768/9/72/74-88	18	Wright New Routemaster	Abellio	QB	211		1
	VH45169/70/72-81	12	Volvo B5LH/Gemini 3	Ldn United	TV	85	02/07/2016	
		58						
July	2513/5/7-21	7	ADL Enviro400H City	CT Plus	HK	26	27/02/2016	5
	12366/7/70-82/5/7/8	18	ADL E40D/Enviro400 MMC	Selkent	PD	53	23/07/2016	
	36617	1	ADL E20D 8.9m/Enviro200 MMC	Selkent	TB	146/336	20/08/2016	
	DE20129-42	14	ADL E20D 10.8m/Enviro200 MMC	Ldn United	TV	265	02/07/2016	
	LT794/5/8/9/801/2	6	Wright New Routemaster	Metroline	W	189		1
	SW2-5	4	Wright StreetDeck	Arriva LN	GR	340	03/09/2016	
	VH45171/82	2	Volvo B5LH/Gemini 3	Ldn United	TV	85	02/07/2016	
	VH45183-6	4	Volvo B5LH/Gemini 3	Ldn United	FW	65	02/07/2016	
	VH45187-9/94/5/7	6	Volvo B5LH/Gemini 3	Ldn Sovereign	BT	183	03/09/2016	
		62						
August	2534-51	18	ADL E40H/Enviro400 MMC	Abellio	QB	344	20/08/2016	
	12365/8/9/83/4/6/9/90-400	18	ADL E40H/Enviro400 MMC	Selkent	PD	53	23/07/2016	
	36609-16/18-21	12	ADL E20D 8.9m/Enviro200 MMC	Selkent	TB	146/336	20/08/2016	
	SEe4/5/7/9	4	BYD D9UR 12m/Enviro200 EV	Go-Ahead	RA	507/521	27/08/2016	
	SW6-10	5	Wright StreetDeck	Arriva LN	GR	340	03/09/2016	
	VH45190-3/6/8/9	7	Volvo B5LH/Gemini 3	Ldn United	S	94		2
	VWH2213-19/21/2/4	10	Volvo B5LH/Gemini 3	Metroline	HD	140/182	03/09/2016	
		74						

	Fleet numbers		Type	Operator	Garage	Route	Contract Date	
September	10348-50	3	ADL E40D/Enviro400 MMC	Selkent	TL	199	17/09/2016	6
	12401	1	ADL E40H/Enviro400 MMC	Selkent	TL			7
	DEL2155/8/9/63/5/6	6	ADL E20D 10.8m/Enviro200 MMC	Metroline West	ON	487	09/03/2016	8
	LT789/92/800/5	4	Wright New Routemaster	Metroline	W	189	08/10/2016	1
	MHV57-60/3/4/6-9/70/2	12	Volvo B5LH/MCV EvoSeti	Ldn Central	Q	42/185	01/10/2016	
	SEe3/6/8/10-8	12	BYD D9UR 12m/Enviro200 EV	Ldn General	RA	507/521	27/08/2016	
	SLS1/5/7-9/13/4/6/9/20	10	Wright StreetLite DF 9.75m	Arriva LS	N	450	01/10/2016	
	VWH2167-86	20	Volvo B5LH/Gemini 3	Metroline West	UX	114	03/09/2016	
	VWH2187-93/2201/20/3	10	Volvo B5LH/Gemini 3	Metroline	HD	140/182	03/09/2016	
		78						
October	8343-47	5	ADL E20D 9.7m/Enviro200 MMC	Abellio	BC	P13	08/10/2016	
	EH62/5	2	ADL E40H/Enviro400 MMC	Ldn Central	PM	363	12/11/2016	
	LT790/1/3/803/4/6-11	11	Wright New Routemaster	Metroline	W	189	08/10/2016	1
	LT813-9/21-5/8/9/31	15	Wright New Routemaster	Arriva LN	SF	253		1
	MHV23/5/7/8/41	5	Volvo B5LH/MCV EvoSeti	Ldn Central	PM	63	12/11/2016	
	MHV56/62/5/71/3-9/80/2/3-5	16	Volvo B5LH/MCV EvoSeti	Ldn Central	Q	42/185	01/10/2016	
	SEe19/20-29/31	12	BYD D9UR 12m/Enviro200 EV	Ldn General	RA	507/521	27/08/2016	
	SLS2-4/6/10-12/5/7/8/21/2	12	Wright StreetLite DF 9.75m	Arriva LS	N	450	01/10/2016	
	VH45200	1	Volvo B5LH/Gemini 3	Ldn United	S	94		2
	VHR45203	1	Volvo B5LH/SRM	Ldn Sovereign	BT	13		2
	VWH2194/9/2200/3/5/7/9-12	10	Volvo B5LH/Gemini 3	Metroline	HD	140/182	03/09/2016	
	WHV112/4	2	Volvo B5LH/Gemini 3	Ldn General	AF	74/430	19/11/2016	
	WHV143-5/7/50/2/3/6	8	Volvo B5LH/Gemini 3	Ldn General	MW	1	01/10/2016	
		100						
November	1221-37	17	ADL E20D 9.6m/Enviro200	CT Plus	AW	W19	26/11/2016	
	8155-9/61	6	ADL E20D 8.9m/Enviro200 MMC	Abellio	TF	H20	19/11/2016	
	12402	1	ADL E40H/Enviro400 MMC	Selkent	PD	177		6
	DEL2156/7/60/2/4	5	ADL E20D 10.8m/Enviro200 MMC	Metroline West	ON	487	09/03/2016	8
	EH61/3/4/6-9/70-3	11	ADL E40H/Enviro400 MMC	Ldn Central	PM	363	12/11/2016	
	EH74/6	2	ADL E40H/Enviro400 MMC	Ldn General	AF	14	19/11/2016	
	LT820/6/7/32/3/6/7/9/41-3	11	Wright New Routemaster	Arriva LN	SF	253		1
	MHV21/2/4/6/9/30 & MHV31/3-6/9/40/5/6	15	Volvo B5LH/MCV EvoSeti	Ldn Central	PM	63	12/11/2016	
	MHV81	1	Volvo B5LH/MCV EvoSeti	Ldn Central	Q	42/185	01/10/2016	
	SEe30/2-6/8/40/1	9	BYD D9UR 12m/Enviro200 EV	Ldn General	RA	507/521	27/08/2016	
	VWH2202/4/6/8/26/7/9/30 & VWH2231-8/40/1	18	Volvo B5LH/Gemini 3	Metroline	HD	140/182	03/09/2016	
	WHV113/5-9/20-4/6/7/9/30 & WHV131/2/4/58	19	Volvo B5LH/Gemini 3	Ldn General	AF	74/430	19/11/2016	
	WHV146/8/9/51/5	5	Volvo B5LH/Gemini 3	Ldn General	MW	1	01/10/2016	
	WS67-9	3	Wright StreetLite DF 10.8m	Ldn General	PL	39	19/11/2016	
		123						
December	8160	1	ADL E20D 8.9m/Enviro200 MMC	Abellio	TF	H20	19/11/2016	
	EH75/7/9/80/1/3/5/7/92	9	ADL E40H/Enviro400 MMC	Ldn General	AF	14	19/11/2016	
	LT846/9/51/4/7/9/62/5-7	10	Wright New Routemaster	Ldn Central	NX	21		1
	MCS01-09	9	Mercedes Citaro-K 10.6m	Quality Line	EB	413	03/12/2016	
	MHV32/7/8/42/3/7/8/50-55	13	Volvo B5LH/MCV EvoSeti	Ldn Central	PM	63	12/11/2016	
	MHV61	1	Volvo B5LH/MCV EvoSeti	Ldn Central	Q	42/185	01/10/2016	
	SEe37/9/42/3/5/7/9	7	BYD D9UR 12m/Enviro200 EV	Ldn General	RA	507/521	27/08/2016	
	VHR45204/5/8	3	Volvo B5LH/SRM	Ldn Sovereign	BT	13		2
	VWH2195/228/39/42/3	5	Volvo B5LH/Gemini 3	Metroline	HD	140/182	03/09/2016	
	WHV125/8/33/5/41/61	6	Volvo B5LH/Gemini 3	Ldn General	AF	74/430	19/11/2016	
	WHV154/7	2	Volvo B5LH/Gemini 3	Ldn General	MW	1	01/10/2016	
		66						
TOTAL for the Year		**942**						

Notes: 1 LT conversion   2 Upgrade   3 Enviros ordered for route 35, EvoSetis for route 40, but a pool arrangement applied from Day One
4 Short NRM for running on restricted routes   5 B/fwd from 25th June   6 PVR incr.   7 Top-up to general allocation   8 Entered service at UX

MIscellaneous Vehicles (demonstrators & secondhand)

	Fleet number		Type	Operator	Garage	Route	
16/04/2016	WS11	1	Wright StreetLite WF 8.8m	Ldn United	TV	various	9
19/07/2016	WS65	1	Wright StreetLite DF 10.2m	London Central	NX	108	10
02/08/2016	OM1	1	Optare MetroDecker	London Central	BX	486	
07/10/2016	WHV111	1	Volvo B5LH/Gemini 3	London General	MW	1	
05/12/2016	MCS10	1	Mercedes Citaro 10.6m	Quality Line	EB	413	11
26/09/2016	[LJ16 EZS]	1	BYD K8UR 10.85m	Ldn Central	Q	360	12

Dates shown are first day in service

9   Then on loan to Quality Line (EB) for route 463 from 28th June
10   Then (Q) for P5 from 24th August, and 360 from 3rd November
11   Taken "on loan" for 413. Date is first day for Quality Line
12   Spent one day with HCT in September, but expected to go to Camberwell for route 360

Waiting in the Wings

THIS is a summary of outstanding vehicles at the 31st of December, and those which are imminent for new contracts in early 2017. Unless there are more unexpected delays, you should have seen many of them on the road by the time this is published.

		Routes	Notes
8162-5	WS	U9	
DEL2161	WJ	487	1
EH78/82/4/6/8/9/90/1/3-9/100-112	AF	14	
EH113-130	Q	42	
LT830/4/5/8/40/4	SF	253	
LT845/7/8/50/2/3/5/6/8/60/1/3/4/68-74	NX	21	
MHV44/9	PM	63	
SEe1/2/44/6/8/50/1	RA	507/521	
VH45201/2	S	72	2
VHR45206/7	BT	13	
VWH2196-8/2225	HD	140/182	
WHV136-40/2/159/60/2-7	AF	74/430	
WS66/70-4	PL	39	

1 Likely to join the rest of its diverted batch on Uxbridge routes
2 Seconded to Kingston University work until "spring 2017"

2017 Contracts

2522-37	ADL Enviro 400H City	HK	388	21/1/17
8166-70	ADL E20D 8.9m/Enviro200 MMC	TF	H26	7/1/17
12403-425	ADL E40H/Enviro400 MMC	BW	277	25/2/17
36622-631	ADL E20D 8.9m/Enviro200 MMC	TL	273	14/1/17
AE20-27	ADL E20D 9.7m/Enviro200 MMC	SM	W9	4/2/17
DEL2244-65	ADL E20D 10.8m/Enviro200 MMC	AH	235	7/1/17
HA20-53	ADL Enviro 400H City	BN	133/333	21/1/17
HV201-225	Volvo B5LH/Gemini 3	AR	259	25/3/17
HV226-248	Volvo B5LH/Gemini 3	CT	242	25/2/17

LT Conversions

LT875-902	Route 76	NP	25/3/17	(originally 28th January)
LT903-953	Routes EL1, EL2 & EL3 (formerly 387)	RR	18/2/17	

Below: Despite the numbers on the blinds, these are some of the route 21 allocation in temporary storage at West Ham in December. LT874 appears to have a ticket machine and Oyster readers. *Photo: Dave Jones*